Vicente sat on the   was really nothing more than a room built under the ~~~~. He looked at the rough-hewn wood sided walls and the concrete floor. "Might as well have bars," he mumbled as he moved toward the door. He stepped out just enough to see the house and his parents getting in the car to leave. Inwardly he felt fear though it wasn't the same fear as he had felt a couple of days earlier in Los Angeles when Slider had told him that the rival gang was actively looking for him and Raul. In truth, that was the reason he had agreed to come to spend two weeks in the desert. When his mom and dad suggested a drive to Roswell he made a show of resistance but was secretly anxious to get away for a while. The fear he felt at this moment had more to do with uncertainty. He didn't know what the future held and now he was a thousand miles from home with people he didn't know.

His strategy was to play the hard case, to prove to anyone he might meet that he was tough enough to make it through any situation. He vowed to never let his inward fear show. No matter what came his way he'd be strong. He could do two weeks easy enough.

He leaned at the corner of the barn and heard the car doors slam and the engine start. He watched the Oldsmobile leave the driveway and disappear in the scrub brush and mesquite trees. Vicente returned to the room to sit on his bed. He held his hand to his forehead and even though he wanted to be tough he admitted inwardly that he was scared. He longed for the early days when he and his parents and brother would sit on the porch and shell peas from his mom's small garden in the backyard. They would talk of baseball and school, cars and current events. For an instant he was back there. He could feel the afternoon coolness of the breeze. He closed his eyes and remembered his mom's smile. It had been a long time since she had smiled at him that way.

He shook his head and pushed the memories away.

He angrily stood then turned and kicked the wall. The pain was intense and only served to make him angrier. He was mad at life and mad that things never went his way. "Two weeks," he spat through gritted teeth. "Two weeks then back home. I'm tough enough. I can make it."

A Good Man Gone

Book Four of

Pardner's Trust

Randall Dale

Horizons West Publishing   Safford, Arizona

ISBN:9780986134869

To contact the author

or to order additional copies of this book

www.randalldale.com

Library of Congress Control Number: 2016957615

Printed November 2016 in the

United States of America

One boy is good help, two boys are no help and three boys are like a good man gone. – Old cowboy saying

Part One

A Time to Give

Chapter 1

Eight years earlier

The truck had been old forever. When it was new, many years before Juan came to own it, it was a tan color but the west Texas sun had turned what remained of that color to a rusty brown. The two front fenders had been replaced with parts from long ago wrecked models. One was green and the other blue making for an interesting and ugly mode of transportation.

Rosalinda sat in the passenger seat while Juan drove recklessly toward Carla's house. Their five children were at the home place between San Angelo and Abilene. It was a small but tidy home constructed of whatever Juan had been able to scavenge at the time. They held no title but the owner of the land allowed them to stay there in return for keeping the windmill and pump in good repair though it was not a full-time job. Juan was periodically employed as a day worker on the local farms and ranches but because he, his wife and children had all come to the United States illegally they tried as much as possible to stay out of sight. Each of the previous five children, four boys and one girl, had been born in Mexico without the aid of a doctor and the couple decided to have this baby at home also because of the fear of being deported if they went to the hospital in San Angelo.

"*Apúrate*! Hurry," screamed Rosalinda in Spanish. One hand gripped her abdomen while the other pushed hard on the dashboard to her front and her feet pushed hard on the floorboard.

Juan had the pedal all the way to the floor as he squinted into the blazing afternoon sun. "*Un poco tiempo*," he blurted as the truck dipped into a wash then bumped up and over the opposite side before sliding through a turn in the dirt road. Carla's house was coming into view.

Carla, who had been watering her garden, looked up at the sound of gravel spraying and an engine roaring. She immediately recognized the truck and knew right away that something must be wrong for the dangerous approach. The truck skidded to a stop with the radiator hissing.

She had helped Juan and Rosalinda several times in the past with various medical emergencies that came from having five children all born within a year of each other. From scrapes and bruises to two broken bones, she had been the closest the family had come to a doctor or hospital. She had been a nurse until retirement and had gotten acquainted with the Reyes family in a most unusual way. They had appeared as if from thin air on the day she moved to the small, ultra-rural and completely off-grid house she now called home. The couple had helped her move her belongings then refused payment before disappearing in the old truck.

"Es una problema," yelled Juan while jumping out the door and running to the other side. Carla spoke enough Spanish to understand and every conversation she had with the couple consisted of half English and half Spanish. He opened the door with a savage jerk and grunted as he carefully lifted his pregnant wife from the seat. He followed Carla into the house and to the couch.

Rosalinda's face was contorted in the pain of an intense contraction.

"What's the problem?" asked the nurse. She knew the woman had been able to deliver five babies at home with no issues.

"The time is too much," answered Juan in Spanish then continued in accented English. "The baby no come seence jesterday."

The contraction passed and Carla noticed Rosalinda trying to relax as much as possible. When it appeared as though she might be able to speak Carla asked, "When did you start labor?"

"Yesterday, 2:00 o'clock," came the gasped reply.

The friend thought quickly. Twenty-six hours. "My gosh! Have your contractions been this intense the whole time?"

Rosalinda could only nod.

"We have to get you to the hospital. I'm not equipped to handle something like this." As she said it she was thinking of the fastest way. She glanced at the couple, the husband kneeling at his wife's side holding her hand while she lay on the couch. Both shook their heads then Rosalinda wailed—her muscles stiffening as another contraction gripped her entire body.

The nurse knew there would be no convincing them so she took charge calmly and efficiently. While waiting for the contraction to pass she ordered the husband, "Juan, go to the bathroom and get me some towels from under the sink then go to the kitchen and get me a pan of hot water." He left in a rush. As the contraction subsided she talked to the wife, "Rosalinda, kneel here on the floor. You can rest your head and shoulders on the couch if you like."

Thirty-five minutes later the nurse quickly passed a tiny infant to the father then returned her attention to the mother. The delivery had been far from routine. The stress and the pain caused Rosalinda to pass out. She fell from her kneeling position and slumped to her side on the floor with her mouth lolling open and drool escaping.

"Don't you give up on me," shouted Carla. She quickly rubbed the chubby, sweaty face then let her fingers find a pulse on her patient's neck. The pulse was there and surprisingly strong. The nurse breathed a sigh of relief. She looked at Juan, noticing the worried expression. She nodded with an exhausted smile.

Rosalinda's eyes fluttered open. She had been washed and lay on the floor, her head on a pillow and a blanket covering her. Carla noticed the awakening. "There you are. How are you feeling?"

"*Tengo sed.* Thirsty," admitted the young mother.

Carla smiled. "That's a good sign. You have a new baby girl. She looks just like her dad."

Rosalinda weakly returned the smile with a nod. "Juanita," she declared, and the name stuck.

*** Present day March

The teacher stood in front of the senior English class waiting for the tardy bell to ring and the students to pay attention. His eye was drawn to Gabriella sitting comfortably and attentively at her desk. She watched him intently with her huge, dark eyes. A pleasant, half-smile was on her high-cheekboned face and her long, dark hair hung straight down her back. Her clean but worn hand-me-down clothes hung on her thin body.

He had been at this small high school for the past 12 years and had seen students come and go but Gabriella was somehow different from any in the past. She was smart, very smart, but he had seen smart students before. She was pretty but that wasn't it either. As he thought about it he decided she was hungry. Hungry for knowledge and a better future. *Too bad,* he thought with a small frown.

Everyone in the valley knew the family had come illegally from Mexico somewhere around fifteen years earlier but it didn't matter. They were a hard-working, honest part of the community respected by all. They had an endearing knack to be the first to volunteer if help was needed and somehow always knew when and where to show up.

Gabriella's brothers had all graduated from this rural high school and gone on to jobs on various ranches and farms in Texas and her younger sister, Juanita, was in the fourth grade. Gabriella seemed different from her brothers. They had been smart too but she obviously wanted more. The teacher knew she wanted to attend college and if she had been a legal resident a scholarship would have undoubtedly been offered, but, fear of discovery and possible deportation made applying to college nothing more than a dream for the poor, unfortunate girl.

***

The March sun peeked from the clouds in the pleasant, west Texas valley. Thirty-two-year-old Ricky, bundled in a quilted coat and black felt hat pulled tight on his head against the cool morning breeze, sat on his favorite horse, Pardner, black as night and 18 years old. It was in the early morning air at the far west end of the ranch located between Abilene and San Angelo. He looked toward the house that sat serenely under the crimson clouds of sunrise hoping for but not quite seeing the greening of the grasses. This was a good ranch with gramma grasses thick and ever-present. A partial smile turned the corners of his lips up at the realization that it was too early for the new growth because spring had not yet arrived, nevertheless, out of habit as a rancher, he was always looking for the greening of the grass. His grin expanded at the thought that he, Ricky Richardson, a poor boy from Clovis, New Mexico, actually owned a ranch–and not just any ranch, but one of the best family sized ranches in West Texas.

The saddle creaked as he turned to squint at the sun slowly making its ascent in the eastern sky. He had one more stop on the way home. He started Pardner out at a lope toward a giant oak tree near the top of a hill a quarter mile south of the ranch house. At the crest of the hill close to the tree he stopped in the early morning sun to gaze at the well-kept, white picket fence that surrounded seven headstones. The ranch cemetery, legal and registered in the county and the state, held the remains of persons associated with the ranch. The first of the graves dated back to the early 1900s but the two most recent belonged to the immediate past owners of the ranch.

Ricky stopped to pay his respects but the visit always made him melancholy. The old couple had once been young like he and Jessie but as time marched on they became old. Ricky realized that he too would follow in their footsteps, though that eventuality seemed so very distant. Still, it was comforting to know that he, as well as Jessie, would have a place to rest on this ranch he loved so much. He tipped his hat in respect to the dead then turned his horse and rode through the junipers to the house at a half-trot.

***

A couple of hundred miles to the west, the Roswell, New Mexico early morning sun shone brightly on Román's back as he leaned into the water trough at his ranch. His pants were tucked into his boots and he was ankle deep in mud and muck while attempting to fix the leak from the float and valve that had caused the wet, nasty conditions. Across from the narrow, steel trough, his hired hand Scott leaned in to hold the float assembly to allow Román to insert the cotter pin. With a pair of pliers from his back pocket, the slightly built ranch owner bent the pin to hold the float in place. Both men stood from their leaning. Román glanced at the big boy who returned the gaze with a smile.

"*Esta bien,*" said the ranch owner with a wink and nod. He watched with pleasure the happy countenance on the boy's face and decided that if no one knew his history of trouble with the law they would never guess that the young man had started at his ranch as an agreement with the Roswell, New Mexico probation department. The probation term was completed but the boy had agreed to stay and work and was making a good hand.

"Yes, *Patrón,*" readily agreed the 6'6" teenager with broad shoulders and thick neck. Román smiled at the horrendous accent. He had been trying to teach the boy some Spanish but no matter how much he explained and coached, the youngster just couldn't seem to say the words correctly.

Both men turned and squinted into the early morning sun as they heard a truck bouncing over the rutted ranch road. Román frowned as he recognized his older ranch truck and saw his wife in the driver's seat. He wondered why she would be driving to the windmill. There must be a problem and the thought caused concern.

The brakes squealed in protest as the truck came to a stop nearby. Román's boots made a sucking sound as he stepped from the mud and quickly over to the truck. "What's wrong, Lupita?"

The small, olive-skinned woman with high cheek bones and an angular face glanced from her husband to Scott who respectfully waited at the water trough out of hearing range. She returned her focus to Román. "The Probation Office just called. They want you to call them right away."

He frowned. "What could they want?"

She shook her head and shrugged.

"Okay, then. We're finished here anyway." He opened the truck door and took his wife's hand as he turned to the boy, noticing again how massive and muscular he was. The call must have something to do with him. "Scott. You drive the old truck back and Lupita can come with me. We'll meet you at the house."

"Yes, *Patrón*."

Román and Lupita got in the new truck while Scott jumped in the old ranch truck for the drive back to the headquarters.

At the house, the ranchman dialed the phone.

"Probation." The woman's voice sounded bored and tired even though the day had just begun.

"This is Román Martinez. I was told to call."

"Hold please," came the short reply.

"Hello, Román. Kerry here. So glad you called."

"Hi, Kerry." He was already tired of the chit-chat. "Is

13

there a problem?"

The probation officer replied, "Well... ."

The pregnant pause was unsettling. The ranch owner sat in an oversize leather recliner and tapped his stocking foot. He had taken off the muddy boots at the back door. "Well, what? Either this is about Scott or you have another boy you want me to take in."

"I'm afraid it's about Scott. We got a call this morning from the Sheriff's Office about a burglary last night. Someone saw a big boy at the scene about 10:00 o'clock. One of the detectives remembered Scott from his trouble last year and wanted to know if he was still around. I told them he was and that I'd check to see where he was last night."

Román breathed a sigh of relief. "He was here with me last night. We watched a college basketball game together. It didn't finish until almost 11:00 o'clock. Whoever they saw definitely was not Scott."

"I'm glad to hear that. You sure have a way with those boys and we're glad you're willing to take them in."

Román breathed deeply at the thought of the boys he had helped. He had started taking boys in nearly 15 years earlier. He gave them a job and a place to live. He remembered the first young man, Carlos, who he had helped as a favor to a probation officer. Carlos had turned his life around and became a fine young man and a model citizen. He was a husband and father now and still stayed in contact with Román.

Others had come and gone over the years. Some had responded to his efforts to teach them responsibility and work ethic, some had not. Román watched in his mind as he recalled their faces. He felt remorse for the ones that had not taken advantage of the help he tried to give, but at the same time, he felt great happiness at the numerous successes.

"I appreciate that but you know it's my pleasure. Keep me in mind when you get another good boy that just needs some solitary ranch time."

"You can be sure we'll do that. I'm glad Scott's off the hook. He's a good boy."

"Yes he is," agreed Román. "Yes he is."

Chapter 2

Later that night a thousand miles to the west, three youths strolled nonchalantly down the intermittently lighted sidewalk in East Los Angeles. The gentle breeze occasionally carried small bits of trash and small billows of dust clouds along the sidewalk. The boys wore black shirts and Oakland Raider ball caps pulled low. Their baggy pants sagged and each had to reach periodically to pull them up just enough to keep them from falling down. They occasionally stopped to look through the bars and into the windows of the shops on the street and kept up a lively, friendly banter amongst themselves in English, Spanish and slang.

They each turned to watch as an old, black Pontiac GTO drove by slowly. It was the only car on the street at that late hour, low to the ground and the roar was loud in the almost midnight stillness as the driver gunned the engine. The boys on the sidewalk watched the car carefully as it rolled by at a crawl. Suddenly there was a flash accompanied by a loud report. Vicente felt the whip of the bullet as it passed his left ear and crashed through the glass of the window immediately behind. He and his friends ducked and hid as the car squealed tires leaving in a hurry.

The oldest of the boys, 19 years old, pulled a gun from his waistband. He fired four quick shots toward the retreating car and saw the rear window shatter. Vicente watched in horrified fascination to see the brake lights come on and the car veered to the right then made a quick, tire squealing U-turn in the vacant street.

"Let's get outta here," yelled the shooter.

The boys turned and ran, each holding their pants up with one hand. The car covered the distance quickly as it approached from the rear. The fleeing boys looked for an alley or any other escape option but the storefronts were solid along the block. They heard the shots as the car drew closer and occasionally the whine of a bullet caused them to duck their heads. One bullet hit the bricks to their side and ricocheted down the street with an angry scream.

Vicente's friend Rudolfo, the boy with the gun, turned hurriedly as the car came alongside. He fired the two remaining bullets. In his running, Vicente distinctly heard a scream and the cursing of someone in the car, then several shots in close succession. The detonations were different and even in his panic he realized that more than one gun was being fired. He reached the end of the block and turned to sprint down a dark alley followed closely by Raul, his best friend.

In the blackness at the end of the alley they stopped to rest. Hands on knees they breathed in labored, raspy breaths. They searched in earnest toward the street to see if they were being followed by whoever was in the car. As their breathing returned to something resembling normal they cautiously made their way back to the street. Their older friend had not followed into the alley so they wondered where he was. As they approached they cautiously surveyed the empty street and sidewalks, relieved that the car was nowhere in sight.

They turned to study the sidewalk in front of the storefronts they had run past only a few minutes earlier. In the faded light of the faraway street lamp they saw a prone figure slumped and immobile on the concrete. They ran to their friend's side. He lay face down and a thick pool of blood oozed from under the body. It spread dark on the concrete and dripped in small rivulets from the sidewalk down the curb to the gutter.

***

The old, small, two-bedroom house in East Los Angeles sat on a small lot with neighbors close on each side. A short, bent and ugly chain-link fence surrounded the tiny front lawn and a narrow, crumbling concrete walkway led from the sidewalk to the door. A few thin, scraggly flowers grew at the fence and a dead tree leaned precariously against the roof from the neighbor's yard. Vicente had lived there his whole life though since he graduated from high school he seemed to be there less and less.

His older brother had joined the Marines after high school graduation three years earlier so Vicente had the room all to himself. A knock came at the door.

"Come in," he requested.

His mother, a small, thick woman with graying hair pulled tightly and pinned severely in a bun opened the door and stepped heavily into the dark room with walls covered by pictures of low-rider cars. Vicente looked up and she could tell he knew what she wanted to talk about.

"Were you with him?" she asked in a subdued tone. She had just gotten the call from a friend down the street about the death of the neighborhood boy sometime the night before.

"No," he lied. "I was over at Raul's house."

"Are you involved with that gang?" She suspected he was lying though she hoped against hope that he was not. It was time for hard questions and honest answers. He had been a good boy, and still was she decided, though for the past three years he had become distant and defiant. Before that he had been for the most part a good son. There had been issues as he reached his teenage years. She sucked her breath as she admitted that all of her friend's sons had gone through the same defiant stage where parents were dumb and didn't know what was best for their kids. Nevertheless, before that he had been a good boy.

She thought of the picture in the family album of the 12 year-old helping his father in the driveway. Her husband was a good shade tree mechanic and earned extra money for the family by working on cars in his spare time. The picture showed Vicente with a huge smile as he looked toward the camera. By 12 he already knew more about cars than most of the high-dollar mechanics that worked in the auto shops.

"Hi, mom," she could hear him say each day as he returned from junior high school. She tried always to have milk and cookies ready for him and they would sit at the table and talk of school, of friends and life in general. She looked at him now, eighteen years old, sitting at the desk in the sleeveless 'wife beater' white t-shirt and baggy pants.

He answered her question. "No. I don't need no gang." His glare was hard, unyielding and unapologetic and she could see plainly on his face that he was lying. As he stood in undisguised defiance his baggy pants slipped down just enough for her to see the gun stuffed into his waistband.

He had never carried it before that she knew of though she had seen it in his drawer. He noticed her eyes drawn to the gun. He pulled his shirt down to cover the weapon then pushed past her through the open door. She watched in hopeless desperation as he walked out of the house and let the screen door slam with a bang.

As she watched him she sadly shook her head. What had happened to their son? Contemplating the question she thought back and could remember the day, the exact day when he was 14 that caused his defiance to expand out of control. *No*, she quickly thought to herself. *There were two days. Two distinct days. First was the terrible day the two Marines visited.*

***

The winter sun was low in the sky and that Saturday was warm and clear. The front door was open to let the pleasant, Los Angeles breeze in through the screen door that was closed to keep out the incessant gnats and flies that thrived in the warmer, winter climate. Vicente had actually been pleasant that day and had decided to stay home with the family. He sat on the couch eating popcorn from a bowl perched between him and his father, whom everyone called Pete though his real name was Pedro. Vicente's mother, Sylvia, sat on a soft chair on the other side of the room. All three were watching their beloved Lakers and all three were disappointed at the score. It seemed that every time their team started to rally the other team spurted ahead again.

Pete yelled occasionally and slapped his knee and Vicente alternated between sitting on the couch, jumping up and moaning or squatting on the floor with his head covered afraid to watch. During a commercial they all sat and tried to calm themselves.

Through the open door they heard car doors close on the street in front of the house. Sylvia glanced over her shoulder through the door, gasped, then in a gesture of fear and disbelief, brought her hand to cover her mouth. Pete watched, immediately concerned at the reaction of his wife.

"What is it?" he asked while standing from the couch so he could see outside. At the sight of the Marines in their dress uniforms he stopped, slowly blinking and forcing himself to breathe. They approached the door with serious expressions then stood at attention while the closest knocked lightly.

Pete and Sylvia couldn't move. Vicente watched then answered the door with a look of confusion toward his parents.

"Hi."

"Good afternoon. May we please speak with Mr. and Mrs. Zermeno?"

Vicente barely noticed the lack of pleasantries and no smiles. "Sure. Come on in," he invited as he pushed the screen door outward.

The Marines stepped lightly into the front room holding their caps under their arms. "Ma'am. Sir," said the bigger of the two, nodding at each of the parents.

The couple stood staring at the handsome Marine, willing their bodies not to collapse while waiting for the inevitable. They tightly held to one another.

"We regret to inform you that your son, Private First Class Antonio Zermeno was killed in the line of duty approximately 20 hours ago in Iraq. His heroic actions saved most of the rest of his platoon. He was a good Marine and you can be proud. Please accept our deepest condolences."

Sylvia wailed and her knees buckled. If not for the solid grip of her husband she would have fallen. Carefully he helped her to the chair then faced the uniformed men.

"Thank you for coming," he whispered as he took the proffered paper.

The Marine's face softened, then with a nod both turned and stepped out the door and down the sidewalk.

Pete focused on Sylvia, trying without success to console her. He looked up at the sound of Vicente's door slamming shut. The teen stayed in the room until after dark and never mentioned his brother again.

***

She sighed at the remembrance then thought of the second specific day only a few months after Antonio's funeral service. She reminded herself that it was the day Vicente came home wearing a brand new silver and black Oakland Raiders jacket. After the death of his brother he had become increasingly defiant, angry at the world. Until then a solid B student, his grades took a sudden nose dive and he lost all interest in school and sports. On one occasion she had confronted him, reminding him of the good boy he had been, hoping to encourage him to release the anger he held so deeply. The conversation had the opposite effect. He exploded in rage then stormed out of the house. The next days the atmosphere at home was charged with animosity. It had been a terrible week but after he got the jacket things got worse.

***

Vicente, only a few months older than he was on the

day they all tried to forget, stood an inconsequential 5'6"
and was skinny as a rail. He and Raul, only slightly larger,
walked into the bright fall Los Angeles sun from the old,
dark and dank high school building. As they walked down
the steps they were directly behind one of the prettiest girls
in the school. She was a junior and they freshmen but that
didn't keep them from admiring her. She stopped at the
sidewalk for a moment, put her book between her knees to
free her hands then gathered her long, dark hair into a
ponytail and expertly pulled it through the rubber band
three times.

She held the book and smiled at the boys as they
walked past. Suddenly an older, low to the ground blue
metallic Chevy convertible pulled to the curb. She skipped
by the boys and climbed over the door and plopped into the
seat. The driver who wore sunglasses and an Oakland
Raiders cap pulled low and to the side looked at least 19. He
nodded as he observed the boys watching her.

"Do you guys want to come to a party with us?"

The boys looked behind them. Surely the older teen
wasn't talking to them but there was no one there. They
returned their gaze to the man. "Jump in," he suggested.

Vicente thought for the briefest instant. He knew his
mom expected him to go straight home after school each
day but since she had taken a job at the dry-cleaners six
months earlier she never got back to the house till after 6:00
and his dad worked till 7:00. He looked at Raul who
shrugged.

Both then looked at the girl. She was smiling. "Come
on, guys," she said with a motion of her head toward the
back seat. "Let's go."

Neither of the boys wanted to admit that maybe they
didn't want to go so together they stepped over the side and
slid into the back seat. The driver grabbed the shifter knob
in the shape of a skull to put the car in gear. He turned the
welded chain steering wheel and eased onto the road
leading out of the parking lot and into the street beyond.

Chapter 3

In five minutes they arrived at a house not too far from their own neighborhood. The older teen held the girl closely while walking up the sidewalk with the boys following behind. The door was opened before they got to it. Just inside stood a marginally fat 20 something man in a wife beater, baggy pants and a bandanna tied around his head.

"*Hola, esé,*" he greeted the driver. He growled the vowels as he stretched the word. The two slapped hands then finished with a fist bump. The man ignored the girl but looked with undisguised interest toward the boys. "Who are your freends?" He stretched the word again which only added to his accent. He held his hand for a slap.

"Vicente." He got a slap and a fist bump.

"Raul." He got the same.

"Come on in. Welcome to our house," he invited. The last word of every phrase was stretched.

The foursome entered and cold cans of Coke were thrust into the boy's hands. They could hear Spanish music as it blared from speakers in the backyard. There were about 20 people milling about the house and they recognized at least four others from their high school. The rest of the crowd were older, in their late teens or early 20s. Some of the attendees were drinking beer, others Cokes and there were open bags of chips and dip on the coffee table.

The driver and the girl had disappeared so the boys were left standing alone at one of the living room walls. Vicente was feeling uncomfortable until two boys from their high school strolled to their side.

"Hi, guys. Good to see you here. Ain't this a great party?"

Vicente looked around. He had never been to this kind of party and suddenly felt guilty that he hadn't gone straight home. "Sure," he lied.

"Wait till you get to know some of the guys," volunteered the high school senior. "They're really nice." The boy turned, searching for someone, then apparently seeing who he was looking for called loudly, "Slider."

Vicente followed his gaze and watched as a tall, muscular early 20 something man also in a wife beater and wearing sunglasses and a bandanna acknowledged the call. He smiled and drifted their way.

"Hi, guys. Glad you're here. Everybody calls me Slider. What's your name?"

Each of the boys introduced themselves.

The high school senior patted Vicente on his back. "Slider's a good man to know. He's what's called a distributor and he can hook you up with all kinds of cool stuff."

Slider's attention had been momentarily drawn somewhere else so he stood half turned from the group. Vicente noticed a tattoo on the man's hairy back up to his neck ending at his hairline. It was black and dark and looked like an eagle's talon holding the Mexican flag. He felt the first fluttering of discomfort at the situation.

"Ain't that right, Slider?" asked the boy.

The big man turned to rejoin the group with a nod. "It sure is. Wanna see?"

Both boys lifted their palms and shrugged.

Slider led them to a back bedroom where they noticed plastic-wrapped parcels covering the bed. The big man rummaged through them till he found what he was looking for. "Here they are," he said with satisfaction. "I'm guessing about a medium so these should work." He handed each a package.

Vicente placed his half-empty can of Coke on the bed stand to grasp the package in both hands. He could see the Oakland Raiders emblem through the cellophane. He looked up at the man with a questioning look.

"It's yours."

Vicente shook his head. "I don't have any money."

"Don't need no money. Consider it a gift from me. All I ask is that you come by once in a while to visit. We are, after all, friends. Right?"

Vicente rubbed the cellophane then looked at the man again. "Thanks."

They spent the next hour at the party getting acquainted and eating chips and dip while drinking another Coke. The longer Vicente was there the more comfortable he felt. These were good guys and he enjoyed getting to know them but at 5:30 he confessed that he needed to get home.

"I'll drive you," volunteered one of their new friends, the high school senior.

Vicente stepped out of the car wearing the gift even though the Southern California afternoon was warm and no jacket was needed. He arrived just as his mom was getting out of her car.

"That's a nice jacket," she said, her eyes questioning.

"Sure is. I met a guy today who gave it to me. He said I should wear it as advertising for his business."

"That doesn't sound right? It's not a gang is it?"

He could see her skeptical expression and hear the concern in her voice. "It's fine mom. I've made new friends and they're great guys. Trust me. I'm smart enough not to get involved in any gang thing. They're just a bunch of guys that are friends, that's all." He turned his back and walked into the house leaving his mom to carry the groceries. He was young but not completely naïve. He knew it was a gang but he liked the jacket and liked the idea that he had friends.

The next day Vicente proudly wore his new jacket to school. During lunch his newfound friend, the high school senior found him in the cafeteria. "Hey, Vicente. Slider was wondering if you'd be able to help him out this afternoon. He has a delivery he needs to make but he's expecting a customer and has to stay at the house. Would you be able to take the delivery? It's not far, just walking distance."

Vicente's radar raised and the first inklings that he was in deeper than he wanted to be crept icily into his consciousness. He looked at the boy waiting expectantly for an answer. He pushed away the feelings of discomfort. It was just a favor. What harm could it do? "Sure, I guess so."

"Great. Do you remember how to get to the house?"

"Yeah. I can find it."

"Fantastic. Take Raul with you."

Walking to the house took 20 minutes. As they approached and before they could knock, the front door opened. The same almost fat man greeted them by name then took them to the back bedroom where Slider waited.

"Ah. Hello, Vicente. Hello, Raul. Nice jackets." He smiled knowingly. "Thanks so much for coming to help. You guys are life savers." He grasped each of the slightly built boys around their shoulders. He was so big and muscular that he made them feel small but the embrace made them feel needed and accepted.

"All you have to do is deliver this package to this address." He gave them a slip of paper with a neatly written address. He then took them to the front yard and expansively gave directions to the house. Finally he reached into his pocket to give each a five dollar bill. "I don't expect you to do this for free. In fact, if you like, you can deliver for me every day. Just come by after school and I'll have everything ready for you."

When his mom got home late that afternoon he was sitting on the couch watching a mind numbing show on the

TV.

"Hi, Vicente," she greeted. He only grunted in return.

Vicente and Raul visited the house every day after school. Most days they had local deliveries but some days they just lounged around the house enjoying a Coke and chips and dip and getting acquainted with the various people that dropped in.

Slider was experienced at recruiting and his methods were highly successful. He brought the boys into the gang slowly but with practiced expertise. At first it was Coke and chips but by the end of the second week, Vicente was surprised that instead of handing them a Coke, Slider offered a beer instead. The pair looked at each other, both remembering the last beer they had tasted. They had been eleven or twelve and in boyish mischievousness sneaked one of Pete's out of the refrigerator then hid behind a scraggly tree in the backyard. After popping the top Vicente took a small sip then immediately spat it out.

"Yuck," he exclaimed. "That's nasty."

Raul touched his tongue to the opening and lifted the can just enough for a taste. His reaction was the same.

Now the boys, each holding a can, looked at each other with grim determination. With a final glance toward Slider each took a sip and forced it down. By the time the afternoon was over they had each finished their first beer.

A week later Slider called them to the backyard where a group was already assembled. All watched them expectantly when the joint they were passing reached Vicente. He knew what it was but pushed any hesitation aside for fear of coming across as just a kid. After all, he had been able to finish the beer and several more since the first one a week earlier, he would be able to fit in when it came to marijuana also.

The group laughed as he coughed at his first drag so somewhat self-consciously he quickly took another, breathed in the smoke and repressed the urge to cough. The boys and men in the group cheered him on and he proudly

27

passed the joint to Raul. The spiral into the gang increased speed as the weeks rolled by.

In the house one Friday afternoon a group of high school aged boys and 20 something-year-old men gathered around Slider on the back porch. The two newcomers naturally gravitated that way as they felt comfortable with the men and boys that hung around. When Slider saw them approaching he quickly pushed the gathered crowd back so the boys could be part of the group. The gun in his hand glinted blue in the sunlight and looked cold even though the temperature in Los Angeles that day was in the nineties.

"If you guys would like one of these I can hook you up. You never know when you might need to protect yourself. Just say the word."

"Sure," answered Vicente with false bravado. He was fitting in with his newfound friends and didn't want to jeopardize his standing.

Raul noticed the clock. "We have to be heading out. Great seeing you. Thanks for letting us come over."

Slider put his arms around the boys' shoulders and walked with them through to the front door. They stopped at the curb next to the car they had ridden in the very first day. "You boys have been a big help. I've got a real important delivery tomorrow. Would either of you be able to take it? It's a little farther than the deliveries you've made but not so far that you can't go on foot."

The boys looked at each other and both shrugged.

"I guess you could go together," volunteered Slider. "In fact, that may be for the best. Tomorrow's Saturday so you don't have school. Can you meet me here at 10:00 o'clock? I'll pay you $20 each."

"Sure," they said in unison, both becoming more comfortable with their association and both enjoyed have some extra spending money.

The deliveries became more important and more frequent and the boys were absorbed into the gang. Slowly, their dressing style changed and Vicente, in particular, became increasingly rebellious in his home. He was seldom there and when he was present he refused to help his dad with the cars or his mom with any house or yard work. The more his mom worried the angrier he became. The gang had fully embraced him and he had fully embraced the gang.

***

Vicente slammed the door as he left the house that morning after the confrontation with his mother. There had been a time when he would never have lied to her but that time was past. He walked toward Raul's house. He had traveled less than a block when the low riding convertible approached from the other direction. It was the same car driven by the same man that had taken them to Slider's house on the first day almost four years earlier. It stopped at the curb. "Hey, Gear Man," came the greeting. It was his gang nickname that he had gotten when he started working in the chop shop. He quickly became the one the other members called to fix their low-riders.

"*Hola,* Carlos."

"Slider wants to talk with you. Jump in."

Neither spoke during the ride to the house. They were met by Slider as they pulled up. Raul was also there. The fall morning was pleasantly cool but Slider's disposition was exactly the opposite.

"You were with him last night. What happened?"

Raul and Vicente looked at each other. Both shrugged then Vicente spoke. "We don't know who it was. The car just pulled up slow then there was a shot. Rudolfo shot back then we took off running. The car turned around and came after us. That's when he was killed."

Slider swore in Spanish. The veins on his neck were popping out and he looked as though he might have a stroke. "I hear it was the 82nd streeters and I hear they're looking for you two now. The shots Rudolfo fired hit two of their guys and one is probably going to die. If he does you two had better watch your backs."

The boys looked at one another, each remembering the fear they felt the previous evening. Vicente shivered at the thought.

"But we didn't shoot," protested Raul.

"Don't matter. You were there. If they come to our turf we'll take care of them but if you guys aren't close we can't protect you."

Vicente was scared but he couldn't let on. "Let them come," he hissed, patting the front of his pants where the gun now rested behind his waistband. "I ain't scared of them."

Both boys hung around Slider's house for the rest of the day. Though neither admitted it, they were scared. Finally, at dark, they were driven to their respective homes. Vicente walked in. He saw his mother on the phone. *Good*, he thought as he walked directly to his room where he shut and locked the door.

He peeked through the curtains to the street in front of the house. On any other night he wouldn't have given the empty street another thought. Tonight, though, the thought of someone coming after him with a gun weighed crushingly on his young shoulders. He sat heavily on the bed, admitting to himself that he was terrified. He had never been in trouble but now he was in more trouble than he could have ever imagined. He thought about the preceding four years. Though he had lied to his mother he realized he was in the gang and in deeper than he wanted. He confessed inwardly that he had been in denial from the beginning. He had tried to imagine that they were just a bunch of good friends but down deep he knew all along. Delivering the packages had been one thing but when he got 'transferred' to work in the chop shop he became a full-fledged gang-banger.

Still, they were a quiet gang living in their neighborhood. They didn't encroach on the neighboring gang and the arrangement was mutual. Theirs was a money-making gang and that's where their efforts were spent. In the four years since joining there had not been a single fight. At least there hadn't been until the previous night. Now someone wanted to kill him and Raul.

He removed the ugly, snub-nosed piece from his waistband and turned it over in his hands before placing it carefully on the dresser. If the truth was told, he hated it and wished he would never have let Slider talk him into buying it.

He remembered his growing up years. He'd been naïve but happy. *Why do we have to grow up?* he questioned silently.

***

His mother was in the kitchen still on the phone. "*Madre de Dios,*" she whispered into the mouthpiece. Her face drained of all color as she sat heavily on the rigid, wooden kitchen chair. She continued in Spanish. "He told me he wasn't there."

The voice on the phone was of her good friend, the same one who had called earlier in the day to tell the news of Rudolfo. "He was there and now the other gang is looking for him. One of their guys died and I hear they've sworn revenge on him and Raul. "You should get him out of town for a while."

She hung up the phone then rested her head on the table. She questioned again what had happened to their son. She looked up as she heard the sound of the car through the opened windows. Her husband was parking the Oldsmobile on the curb at the street. She walked out the front door to slide into the passenger seat. She sat quietly at first, wringing her hands.

He reached to touch her lovingly on the arm. "What is it?" he asked.

She focused on him with tears running down her cheeks. "Vicente's in trouble. It's the rival gang." She watched him frown and hang his head before telling all she knew.

They sat in silence for several minutes. Finally, he

31

asked, "What can we do?"

She had been anticipating that question and had been thinking of possible solutions.

***

At the rural ranch house outside of Roswell, New Mexico, Román took the phone from Lexi, his daughter, now 13 years old going on 18. *Where has the time gone*? he questioned himself.

"Hello."

"*Hola*, Román," said the voice on the phone. Román cocked his head. He had heard the voice but couldn't quite remember where. The voice continued in Spanish. "This is your cousin, Sylvia, in Los Angeles."

"Well, Hi, Sylvia. I haven't talked to you in years. How are you today?" asked Román, also in Spanish, wondering why Sylvia was calling and hoping it wasn't bad news.

"We're fine but we need a favor."

"Oh? What can I help you with?"

"It's our son, Vicente. He is running with a bad crowd and we need to get him away from Los Angeles. We were hoping he could come live with you in Roswell for a while. We don't know where else to turn."

Román was silent as he recalled the last time he had seen Vicente. It had been four or so years earlier, at the funeral. At that time the boy was 14 or 15 and though he was sullen at the funeral Román remembered him from earlier times as a laughing, polite boy with a ready smile.

"*Hola, allí*. Are you there?" came the voice from the phone, bringing Román back from his day dreaming.

"I'm here," he answered, getting back to the conversation. "Is Vicente in trouble with the law?"

"No, but if we don't get him out of here soon, he will be." Then, after a pause, she added, "or worse."

Román understood. Sometimes in bad crowds, the law was preferable by far to some of the other possibilities. "When can you be here?"

"Two days."

"I'll be looking for you," he said, hoping that this would turn out to be a success while trying to suppress an uneasy feeling that had ominously settled in his chest.

Chapter 4

Ricky drove his truck down from the mesa where he had been checking on a windmill on the west end of the ranch. From the higher vantage point he saw the school bus bringing Jimmy Ray and Jewell home. He absently checked the digital clock on the dash of the four-wheel-drive Dodge and smiled. "Right on time," he said aloud though he was the only one in the truck. It was Friday so that meant he would have his son's help for the weekend.

He thought with satisfaction of his twelve-year-old son Jimmy Ray. He was just now getting old enough and big enough to be of real help around the ranch, something Ricky had been looking forward to for several years. The rancher smiled at the thought of Jimmy Ray as a small boy and how he wanted to be with his dad helping at every chance. More often than not he was more in the way than he was a help, but as he grew the help he was able to give was appreciated. Then Ricky frowned at the thought that for the past couple of years the boy didn't act like he wanted to help. Not that he didn't do what he was told, and he was good help, but he didn't seem to enjoy ranch work, which was hard for Ricky to understand.

He parked in the yard 12 minutes later and strolled into the kitchen noticing Jimmy Ray, with black hair and stocky frame like his dad, but delicate facial features like his mom, sitting at the kitchen table eating cookies reading a book about, of all things, sea creatures. Ricky shook his head.

To the father's dismay, the boy was infatuated with the ocean even though he had never seen one. He had read all the available books from the school library and every time they visited Clovis to see his grandma, he checked out more from the library there. It seemed to Ricky that every spare moment for Jimmy Ray was spent reading those dumb ocean books.

Ricky removed his hat and wiped the sweatband while watching his son. "Jimmy Ray, did you feed the chickens?"

Jimmy Ray glanced up. "Uh, no, sir. I forgot."

The father looked at his son, disappointment showing on his face. "You've got to get your nose out of those books and do better about remembering your chores. It's up to us to take care of the animals because they can't take care of themselves."

"Yes sir," said the youngster politely, carefully placing a bookmark to save his place before closing the book.

As Jimmy Ray was leaving, Ricky added, "Tomorrow morning early we'll saddle up so you and I can ride out to Johnny Lyon spring. There are a couple of cows hanging around there that should be having calves any day now. We can check on them."

"Yes sir," came the not very enthusiastic reply. Up until he was nine or so, Jimmy Ray had loved riding the horses with his dad, but the older he got and the more he rode, the riding had become work rather than pleasure. And he and his dad never seemed to have anything to talk about. Not that there wasn't a lot of talking, at least from his dad, because every time they rode, it seemed like he was getting another lecture. No matter what Jimmy Ray did, it was never quite good enough.

That's not to say there weren't times when Jimmy Ray loved riding the horses on the ranch with his dad. His favorite times were when other people came to ride too. When other people were there, especially Bob or Flemming, his dad would tell stories of things he had done, places he had been or horses he had ridden. Jimmy Ray loved hearing about his dad's early years and wondered why his dad never wanted to tell him those stories.

Saturday morning, the father and son breathing white in the frosty air, both in black felt cowboy hats and sheepskin coats, went out to the horse corral to catch the classy dun horse they called Dunny. Ricky had started Dunny as a three-year-old eight years earlier. It was at the same time that Jewell, Jimmy Ray's sister, was born. As the years passed and Jimmy Ray grew, Dunny became his horse.

Jimmy Ray stood next to the dun and rubbed the horse's cheek as he voluntarily lowered his head to accept the halter. The boy buckled it on then led the good-looking horse over to the tack room. He let Dunny stand as he stepped up on the concrete pad and into the tack room to get the curry comb and brush. He spent a minute getting the dust and dirt from the horse before returning for the saddle blankets. He carried them back outside, only to see his dad brushing the horse again.

Ricky looked at his son as he brushed down the inside of the horse's back leg. "Son, you've got to take pride in your horses. When you brush them, make sure to take the time necessary to get all the dirt off the whole horse, not just his back."

Jimmy Ray looked down. "Yes sir," he replied.

Ricky pushed the classy dun closer to the concrete step so Jimmy Ray could reach to put the blankets and eventually the saddle on. The boy was growing, but like his father at this age, he was small and not yet tall enough to saddle the big horse from the ground. The foot thick concrete pad gave him the height he needed to throw the heavy saddle onto the horse's back.

Ricky mounted Pardner, who had been standing three legged, relaxed at the side of the barn with a saddle on his back. Pardner was Ricky's favorite horse, the best horse he had ever ridden. There had been some rough times when they were first getting acquainted almost twelve years earlier. The horse had been a bucker, but as trust developed between them, Ricky and Pardner became a team. The horse was getting some age on him so he was ridden only sparingly, mostly as a cutting horse in the corrals during round-up.

The young father sat comfortably in the saddle, waiting for Jimmy Ray to pull the cinch tighter. The boy grabbed the saddle strings, then leaned back to put his left foot in the stirrup. He was able to pull himself into the saddle and began to turn the horse toward the gate leading out to the pasture. One look at his dad pulled him up short.

"Now, Son," Ricky began with a look of disappointment. "How many times have I told you to mount with both hands on the saddle horn? Get off and try it again."

"Yes sir," answered the boy with his head down, doing what he was told. He stood again on the concrete pad, then stretched both hands to the saddle horn. He could reach it, barely. He jumped and pulled, holding himself at the horse's side as his left foot searched for the stirrup. When he finally found it, he was able to step onto the horse. He looked toward his dad, hoping for a sign of approval, but Ricky had already started Pardner toward the gate. Jimmy Ray's gaze followed his dad. He shook his head, then coaxed the dun into a walk to silently follow.

As they rode toward the gate, neither noticed eight-year-old Jewell, watching them longingly through the sliding glass door of the house. After they were out of sight, Jewell walked into the kitchen where her mom, Jessie, was cleaning the table and counter from breakfast. "Mom?"

"Yes, Dear," replied Jessie as she carried the dishes from the table to the counter.

"When will I get to ride with dad?"

Jessie lovingly looked at her daughter. She knew that more than anything in the world, Jewell wanted to be able to go on rides with her dad, but her health would not allow it. She had been born prematurely so her lungs had not properly developed. She had spent seven weeks in an incubator at the Clovis hospital and seemed to be fine, until at two years old, an infection had damaged her delicate lungs such that with any exertion or any dust, severe coughing episodes left her incapacitated. "Maybe after the next rain we can all go out for a short ride."

Jewell stepped closer to give her mom a hug, then slowly climbed the stairs. She liked to sit on the balcony of her parent's room. As she sat there, she could see the two riders topping a hill a half mile away, riding toward Johnny Lyon spring. As the riders disappeared she noticed a dust cloud on the county maintained dirt road. The juniper trees prevented her from seeing the old Chevy truck that was raising the dust as it approached. Their ranch was at the end of the road and traffic was sparse. She watched carefully wondering who it might be and was happily surprised when the old truck with different colored fenders came into view. She hurried down the stairs while at the same time being careful not to overexert which would lead to a coughing fit.

She joined her mom in the driveway just as the truck rolled to a stop with brakes squeaking and a sputter and wheeze from the engine. A rotund Mexican woman exited with a huge smile before slamming the door with a flourish. From the passenger side came her two daughters, Gabriella, a 17-year-old high school senior and eight-year-old Juanita.

"Hello, Rosalinda," greeted Jessie to the driver. I'd forgotten you were coming today. So good to see you."

The woman laughed. Her face was creased and round and though she looked much older than her 49 years with her graying hair tied in a tight bun, her perpetual expression of delight was always a welcome sight. "Ju know I come each first Saturday of the month."

Jessie joined in the laughing with a shrug, remembering eight years earlier how this woman, pregnant at the time, and her husband along with their daughter and four sons had shown up to help the new ranch couple move in. They were suddenly there, carrying boxes and helping move furniture. Their help had been appreciated though Ricky and Jessie didn't know them and had not requested any help. At the end of the moving, the family loaded into the same truck with the mismatched fenders, boys in the back and mom, dad and daughter in the front, laughing as they stubbornly refused offers of pay. They were gone with a wave leaving a grateful but bewildered Ricky and Jessie standing on the front porch.

Ricky learned later that the family lived in a small house ten miles away and survived by day working for farmers and ranchers in the area. It seemed they had a knack for knowing when help was needed throughout the valley though as was the case with the moving assistance, pay was often refused. In no time Jessie had hired Rosalinda to help with house chores and the arrangement became more or less permanent with the woman coming once a month. The help was welcome and the young couple always tried to pay well to help the kind-hearted family. Juan, the dad had since started working full-time for a rancher across the valley and the boys were all grown and gone leaving only Juanita and Gabriella at home.

Jessie watched as her daughter and Juanita gleefully passed through the kitchen to Jewell's room where they would play while the women cleaned. She then noticed Gabriella. The girl was getting prettier with each passing month. Her hair was long and dark, hanging straight down her back. She had the darkest eyes and a perpetual, shy smile on her olive-skinned face.

"Hi, Gabriella," Jessie called over the hood of the truck. The girl only nodded but her smile grew.

The three women cleaned and tidied the house, finishing by late morning. Jessie pushed a $100 bill into Rosalinda's hand and smiled warmly at the protestations that it was too much. It was a monthly occurrence and both knew that the pay would not be reduced. Jessie and Jewell waved as the smoke-belching truck backed out of the driveway and sputtered until it was out of sight.

**

After dinner that evening, Jimmy Ray lay on the couch in the living room of the ranch house. His head was on the armrest and behind him was a lamp so he could have adequate light for reading another ocean book. Jessie walked in to sit on the couch next to him. They were alone in the room. He looked up and smiled at his mom.

She rubbed his shoulder. "Your dad said you made a good hand today. He said you ride Old Dunny like a real horseman and he's proud of you."

Jimmy Ray saw the love on his mom's face. He could imagine his dad saying something like that. His only wish was that his dad would say those things to him once in a while instead of picking at him all the time.

Jessie placed her hand on his shoulder. "You know he loves you and he's proud of you, but he's never been one to be able to say what he really feels. I suppose it's always been the way of a father to expect a lot from his son. He's just trying to teach you the best he knows how."

Jimmy Ray nodded at his mother. "Thanks," he sighed.

The phone rang, interrupting the moment. Jessie stepped to it. "Hello."

"Hi, Jessie. This is Román. Is Ricky there?"

"Hi, Román. Sure, he's in the other room. I'll get him."

"Hello Román," said Ricky, picking up the handset from the table. "How in the world are you?"

"I'm good my friend, but I need a favor."

"Sure thing, Román. Whatever you need."

"I've got one of my boys here at the ranch. His name is Scott. He's a good boy and has come a long way. He's a hard worker and very respectful. He's just coming off of probation now but needs to stay away from his former friends for a while longer. I had planned on him staying here for another four months or so, but my cousin called and is bringing her boy. I'm afraid he'll be a handful and Scott doesn't need any more bad influences. You've said in the past that you'd like to be able to help these boys. Would you be willing to take Scott for a time and work him on your ranch? He just turned 18 and has passed the GED so you won't have to worry about school. He just needs a good friend and a place where he can feel needed."

There was no answer for a time. Román waited patiently while Ricky was thinking about what influence a troublesome boy would have on his family. At length, he said, "Let me make sure it's okay with Jessie. When will you bring him?"

"Tomorrow."

"I'll call you right back."

He walked into the living room, noticing Jimmy Ray reading on the couch and Jessie sitting in a chair at the computer table, reading an article on the internet. He stepped to the hallway leading to Jewell's room. "Jewell, Honey, would you come in here please."

Jessie and Jimmy Ray both glanced up from their reading, obviously wondering what was happening. Jewell came into the room, stepped to the couch and waited for Jimmy Ray to sit up so she could take a seat. Jessie moved to a plush, leather-covered rocking chair and Ricky sat in an identical one next to her. The three looked at him expectantly.

He was quiet for a time, stopping to wonder if he was making a bad decision. He looked at each of them. This was a big step and he wasn't sure how they would react. "That was Román on the phone. You know how he takes in young men that are struggling to help them get on the right path. Well, he wants us to bring one here to the ranch and hire him to work. I want to know if it would be all right with you before I say we will. What do you think?"

The two youngsters looked at their mom, instinctively knowing it was her decision. She smiled at the children. When they smiled in return, she focused on Ricky and after thinking for only a short while, said, "After all we have been blessed with, how could we refuse?" Then, as an ever practical mother, she laid out the ground rules. "He can stay in the bunkhouse but he'll eat his meals with us. He'll be expected to listen and obey what we tell him and Jimmy Ray and Jewell are never to be left alone while the boy is here, at least until we get to know him better."

Ricky smiled. He had been thinking the same thing. "His name is Scott and he'll be here tomorrow. Román said he's a good boy and has come a long way. I'm happy we can help him out."

Chapter 5

The multicolored truck rested in the driveway at the Reyes homestead in southwest Texas. Juan, Rosalinda, and Juanita sat around the kitchen table on mismatched chairs while Gabriella read aloud a letter recently received from Pablo, the youngest of the brothers. He had barely turned 20 and was working for a big ranch west of Houston. The parents beamed proudly at the news but Gabriella pursed her lips while looking at the floor. All her brothers had done well in school and there was never a question of their legal or illegal status because Texas state law provided that all children should attend school without regard to citizenship. Unfortunately, thought Gabriella, colleges in Texas didn't look so favorably on illegals and expected out-of-state tuition to be paid if the student couldn't prove legal status. The five boys had gone off and found work which left only Gabriella and Juanita at home. The high school senior carefully folded the letter and replaced it into the envelope. The parents and her younger sister were all smiles but she sighed in disappointment.

"*Qué es*?" What is it? asked her father.

"It's nothing," she answered, always speaking in Spanish to her parents. She passed the envelope to her mother but Rosalinda took her hand as well as the envelope.

"What's wrong, *Mi Hija*?"

The girl was immediately ashamed at the desire to go to college. She had no birth certificate, no driver's license and worst of all, no money to go to college even though the school counselor tried to reassure her that it might be possible. She looked from her mother to her dad then dropped her head in despair. "Today in school they talked of college. If things were different I'd go and become a nurse."

Rosalinda squeezed her daughter's hand before encouraging, "You can go to college."

The girl looked up, frustration plain on her pretty young face. "How, Mama? We are all illegal except for Juanita because she was born here. If I try to go to college they will discover us and deport us. I read the news every day at school. They want to send all illegals back to Mexico but I've never lived in Mexico. I was born there but have lived here my whole life. How can I be sent back to a place I've never really been?"

Her mother patted her hand. "Let's see what we can do," but even as she heard it Gabriella knew there was no chance.

***

It was almost noon on a pleasant, sunny winter day. Ricky, Jessie and Jimmy Ray had been working to clean the bunkhouse to get it ready while Jewell stayed in the house away from the dust. The bunkhouse had been empty for the last two years so a good amount of dust and dirt had accumulated.

They worked until lunchtime then went in to eat a hastily prepared meal. As they were finishing their quick meal they heard through the window screens a truck pulling into the driveway. All four walked out the front door to stand on the porch and wait for Román and Scott to get out.

Through the glinting sunlight on the windshield, they watched as Román smiled and waved from his seat in the truck, then opened the door to exit. Scott got out from his side. All eyes were on him, and there was a lot of him to see. He stood at least six inches over six feet and was muscular and thick. He wore a t-shirt stretched over his huge chest and massive arms.

As they made their way up the sidewalk, the contrast was amusing. Scott, at least 250 pounds and Román, at most 145 pounds soaking wet.

Román made his way to the family, shaking Ricky's hand and hugging Jessie. He shook Jimmy Ray's hand with a comment about how big he was getting, then he knelt in front of Jewell and, holding her hand, said for all to hear, "You're getting as pretty as your mother."

At Jewell's blushing, Román laughed, then stood to introduce Scott. The muscular boy grasped Ricky's hand. "Hello *Patrón*," he said, looking Ricky in the eye.

Ricky suddenly remembered riding on the TC Bar ranch in Clovis, New Mexico many years earlier with Jake and Román and hearing Jake call his mentor *Patrón*. He could remember like it was yesterday, what Román had said, "I have the boys call me *Patrón*. It's Spanish for boss, but it's more than that. It's a boss that cares."

Ricky quickly felt the trust that was to be given him by this big teenager. He vowed to live up to that trust.

***

The Oldsmobile pulled into the yard at 4:00 o'clock in the afternoon. Román and Lupita hurried out to meet their California relatives. Sylvia and her husband exited the car and received hugs of welcome from the ranch couple. Román stepped back, waiting patiently for Vicente to open the back door and get out. When no movement came he turned to Sylvia with a questioning look. She merely shrugged.

After a minute the door finally opened and out stepped the young man in baggy pants, a sleeveless white wife-beater t-shirt and cap pulled low. He was almost identical to Román in height, about 5'8" and if possible even thinner, only about 135 pounds. Román stepped to the youngster with hand extended but the boy merely grunted and looked at the hand with contempt.

Undaunted, Román heartily welcomed him. "Hello, Vicente. So glad to have you here."

"Whatever," sneered the guest as he looked toward the house. "You got anything to eat?"

Lupita stepped forward. "Of course we do and you must be starving from your trip. Come into the house." She waved for him and his parents to follow her.

She served homemade cookies and milk. The California parents expressed thanks but Vicente scowled at the milk. "Don't you have a Coke?"

Lupita glanced at Román. He answered, "If that's what you want we'll get some next time we go to town."

The boy shook his head and grunted. He scooted the chair away from the table and crossed his spindly legs. He loudly ate the cookies and in an act of obvious defiance, glared at Román while he brushed the crumbs from his pants to the floor. He waited for a reaction. When none came he sat up to address the couple he was to stay with. "I only agreed to two weeks. They," he pointed to his parents with a nod of his head, "They said I had to come to get away from some possible danger at home. I agreed but it's stupid. You stay out of my hair and I'll stay out of your hair and let's get this over with. Deal?"

"Vicente," called his mom. "You are a guest here. Please act like it."

"I ain't no guest." He waved his arm at the house. "I'm a prisoner and everybody here knows it."

Sylvia looked toward her cousin with a helpless shrug. He nodded reassuringly. Then, to Vicente, he said, "I think you'll like it here. Everybody needs some fresh air and time away from the city. We'll be friends, you and me."

"Whatever," came the condescending reply.

***

Román stood from the table, expressed thanks to his wife for the cookies then invited Vicente to the bunkhouse. He returned a few minutes later. He, Lupita, Sylvia and Pete retired to the living room. "Tell us what you think we need to know," requested Román.

The California couple briefly sat in silence. With a nod

46

toward each other Sylvia began explaining the situation. She was initially hesitant but her talking was therapeutic. She told it all, holding nothing back.

"He's a good boy and we had such happy times when he and Antonio were younger. Things started getting out of hand after Antonio died. Vicente fell in with a rough crowd and has become insolent and angry. He was involved in a situation with a rival gang and now we hear they want him dead. We had to get him away and we're so thankful you are willing to take him in till this blows over."

Román sat on the couch holding his wife's hand. He nodded his understanding. "He'll be fine here. We're isolated enough and there's work enough to keep him occupied. Does he need some ground rules or should we just smother him with kindness and love?"

The parents looked at each other. Finally, the father responded, "We've tried both and neither seemed to work for us. You decide and we'll support you. We've taken his phone so he won't have contact with anyone back home. We only hope that he'll come around sometime. Thanks for your understanding." He got up and pulled Sylvia to her feet. "We need to get on the road. We have a long drive home."

Román and Lupita stood also. "It's too late to leave today. We thought you would spend the night here. The guest bedroom is already made up for you," she volunteered.

The guests shook their heads and Sylvia spoke, "No. It's better that we leave now without any more goodbyes. Good luck and we'll see you in a couple of weeks."

***

Vicente sat on the bed in the bunkhouse that was really nothing more than a room built under the barn. He looked at the rough-hewn wood sided walls and the concrete floor. "Might as well have bars," he mumbled as he moved toward the door. He stepped out just enough to see the house and his parents getting in the car to leave.

Inwardly he felt fear though it wasn't the same fear as he had felt a couple of days earlier in Los Angeles when Slider had told him that the rival gang was actively looking for him and Raul. In truth, that was the reason he had agreed to come to spend two weeks in the desert. When his mom and dad suggested a drive to Roswell he made a show of resistance but was secretly anxious to get away for a while. The fear he felt at this moment had more to do with uncertainty. He didn't know what the future held and now he was a thousand miles from home with people he didn't know.

His strategy was to play the hard case, to prove to anyone he might meet that he was tough enough to make it through any situation. He vowed to never let his inward fear show. No matter what came his way he'd be strong. He could do two weeks easy enough.

He leaned at the corner of the barn and heard the car doors slam and the engine start. He watched the Oldsmobile leave the driveway and disappear in the scrub brush and mesquite trees. Vicente returned to the room to sit on his bed. He held his hand to his forehead and even though he wanted to be tough he admitted inwardly that he was scared. He longed for the early days when he and his parents and brother would sit on the porch and shell peas from his mom's small garden in the backyard. They would talk of baseball and school, cars and current events. For an instant he was back there. He could feel the afternoon coolness of the breeze. He closed his eyes and remembered his mom's smile. It had been a long time since she had smiled at him that way.

He shook his head and pushed the memories away. He angrily stood then turned and kicked the wall. The pain was intense and only served to make him angrier. He was mad at life and mad that things never went his way. "Two weeks," he spat through gritted teeth. "Two weeks then back home. I'm tough enough. I can make it."

***

There was a knock on the bunkhouse door. The boy inside squinted as he looked at the clock. It read 6:00 o'clock. The knock came again.

"Vicente, breakfast is ready. Come on to the house and we'll eat." It was Román.

The teen slowly rolled out of bed and went to the door. He opened it wearing nothing but boxer shorts. He sneered at the cowboy hat-wearing man. In an effort to project his tough guy attitude he glared at Román and hissed, "Aren't you going to bring breakfast out here?"

His cousin only smiled which infuriated the youngster even more. He pursed his lips then slammed the door and crawled back in bed.

At noon the knock came again. Vicente had gotten up and was dressed but had spent the entire morning in the bunkhouse. There was no TV, no radio and no computer or internet so the hours had dragged by. He opened the door. Román stood smiling holding a plate with two roast beef sandwiches and a glass of what looked like a Coke on ice.

Vicente acted as though he wasn't hungry and for sure he didn't want to let on that he was in any way appreciative. He'd show this dumb cowboy how tough he could be. He stoically took the plate in one hand and the glass in the other then hooked the door with his toe and swung it shut with a slam. He hurriedly set the plate and glass on a small desk in the room and attacked the food. He was starving.

By dark he was about to go stir-crazy. He had not left the room and had read the old Sports Illustrated magazine at least three times. He occasionally peeked out the door to see if Román might be approaching with dinner but was disappointed each time. By 9:00 o'clock he was past starving and decided a trip to the house would be worth it. He ventured toward the house and knocked on the back door. He could see a shadow approaching from inside. He put on his best 'I hate you and I hate being here' expression as the door opened.

He saw Román's smile and was surprised. He had

thought for sure that the ranchman would eventually get mad but the smile seemed genuine and not forced. *What does it take to get under his skin?* He wondered.

"Hi, Vicente. We were hoping you'd join us for supper. It's late and the girls have already eaten and gone to bed but Lupita and I were waiting for you to join us. Please come in."

He stepped back from the door to allow the young man to enter. Vicente noticed three places set at the table and he smelled the delightful aroma of refried beans and freshly cooked tortillas. The youngster took a seat at the table and greedily started on the food.

"Lupita, Vicente has come in for supper," called Román to the back of the house. She came into the room smiling but the guest didn't notice. He was intent on the food and was already wolfing down his second burrito.

The couple sat at the table then held hands. Román spoke, "Vicente, we would like to say grace. Would you join us please?"

The young man didn't look up. He merely shrugged and waved them away while reaching for another tortilla. The couple bowed their heads while Román prayed. He included thanks that Vicente had been able to come to stay. Each crossed themselves then after a smile toward one another, began the evening meal.

Vicente leaned back and burped loudly. He was disappointed that it didn't anger either of his hosts. He studied the couple across the table. They were slightly younger than his parents and he could see a slight familial resemblance the man and his mom shared. If only his parents had been lucky like this man and his wife. They had it so easy. They obviously didn't know what it was like to scratch out a living. At the thought, his hatred grew.

Chapter 6

Scott and Ricky finished breakfast then walked to the barn in the winter sun. They noticed on the horizon, patches of dark clouds that made it appear as though rain might be possible. The nights were cold but the days often warmed because of the southwestern climate. This day was an exception, it was cold and getting colder as the wind increased.

Ricky was not a small man, standing 6'2" and weighing a solid 195 pounds, but next to Scott, he felt small. It wasn't often he had to look up to anyone. As they walked, he explained that the plan for today was to ride through the mountain pasture to check on the cows there. Though he didn't mention it, an additional benefit to the plan was that he hoped to get acquainted with Scott as they rode. Jimmy Ray was in school so the pair would be the only ones riding this day.

Ricky instructed Scott to catch and saddle a tall palomino he had gotten after his surrogate father, Old Jim, had died. Ricky remembered how Old Jim had taken him, as a twelve-year-old boy, under his wing and helped him along. *Maybe I can do the same thing for these wayward boys,* he thought.

Ricky saddled another horse for himself and was happily surprised at how competently Scott saddled and mounted his own. Obviously, Román had taught him a lot. They rode side by side at a half trot toward the pasture,

51

talking of Román. Shortly, the conversation lagged as they had nothing to talk about.

After riding through a wire gate next to a cattle guard, the big teenager waited for Ricky to remount after closing the gate. "*Patrón*," he said, waiting for his new mentor to face him. "Román said I should tell you my story, my whole story. It's not something I'm proud of and I don't like talking about it, but because he told me to tell you, I will. Would you like to know why I was on probation?"

Ricky thought for a moment. He admitted to himself that he was curious but he wasn't going to ask. "If Román thinks I should know then I'm all ears, but you have to know that I'm no saint. I've done plenty of boneheaded things that I am not proud of. The most important thing is that we learn from our mistakes. If you're better today than yesterday, then you're learning to be a man."

An expression of relief came on the big boy's face. "I'm trying to learn that lesson. Thank you, *Patrón*, for letting me stay with you for a few months." After a moment with neither speaking, Scott started his story.

"Three years ago when I was not quite 16, I was a sophomore in high school. I lived for football and was thrilled when the varsity coaches pulled me up from the JV team. I became the starting defensive tackle and our team was doing well. About half way through the season I got sick. It seemed like I just couldn't get my energy back. It was before a big game when two of the senior boys came to me and had me take a pill so I could play better. That pill led to more and more until I was hooked.

"Drugs are expensive so it wasn't long until I was stealing to pay for them. As much as I loved football, I started loving the drugs more. I'm ashamed to admit how stupid I was. I got arrested and put on probation with the stipulation that I stay clean. I tried, I really tried, but it wasn't long before I was on the drugs again.

"When I got arrested the second time, the judge gave me intensive probation. The probation officer is a friend of

Patrón Román, so that's how I ended up there. I've been clean for six months now and I never want to go back."

***

Ricky sat on the bed, watching through the bathroom door as Jessie, in her nightgown, brushed her long, sandy blonde hair. The kids were asleep and Scott was in the bunkhouse. They were alone for the first time that day. Ricky walked into the bathroom to stand behind his wife, wrapping his arms around her waist and stooping to rest his chin on her shoulder. "Have I told you today how beautiful you are?"

She put the brush on the counter then turned to lay her head on his chest and wrap her arms around him. They held each other tightly, enjoying the moment.

"Scott said it was drugs. That's the reason he was on probation."

Jessie looked up. "I wondered if it was something like that." She resumed her position with her head on his chest.

He combed through her hair with his fingers then held her face with both hands. Looking deeply into her dark eyes he asked, "Are you sure it's okay if he stays?" He knew she had been having second thoughts.

Both were quiet for a long time. Finally, she said, "We've been helped by so many people in our lives it's time for us to be the givers. Everyone needs some good things in their lives and maybe we can provide that. He seems to be a good boy. Everything will be fine."

He pulled her to him and kissed her tenderly. "You're the good thing in my life and I love you." They embraced again, each thinking of how blessed their lives were.

***

The Richardson family and Scott sat at the dinner table. Jessie was learning to cook for an army because Scott ate like an army. He was a good boy and a good worker and was fitting in well. That day he and Ricky had ridden to one of the lower pastures to push two cows and their week-old calves through a gate and over to where they belonged.

Early spring round-up was scheduled to start the following Wednesday so they were trying to get everything ready. Together, they had shod the horses, fixed some broken boards at the loading chute and mended fence where needed. Ricky had bragged to Jessie about how much they could accomplish working together. Jimmy Ray was good help, but Scott was older and a lot stronger so he was called on to do more and more. Besides, Jimmy Ray and Jewell caught the bus for the long ride to school at 6:30 every morning and didn't get back home until after 4:30 in the afternoons so Ricky couldn't get much work out of his son.

At the dinner table, Ricky was bragging on Scott. Jessie watched their son. She knew that it seemed to Jimmy Ray that for the past week, all his dad had done was brag about Scott. Scott could do this or Scott could do that. Scott was so strong or Scott was so athletic.

Jimmy Ray ate silently, his head down. He was listening but not joining in the conversation. "Fine," was his answer when his mom asked how school was going.

Jessie could feel his distance. She knew he was feeling left out because of Scott. She was hoping next week would bring a change. Jimmy Ray would get to stay out of school for the week to help with roundup. Once he got to work alongside Scott and his dad, they would recognize his contribution and he would feel better.

***

It was Monday night at the ranch house. Ricky was sitting on the bed in his underwear. Jessie was standing in a nightgown at the bathroom sink wiping it down after brushing her teeth. Ricky stood then sauntered into the bathroom to stand behind his wife. "I think Scott will be a big help with the round-up. He's a fast learner and is making a pretty good cowboy."

She turned. "I'm glad you're getting along so well with Scott. I like him too, but you have to remember you have Jimmy Ray that wants to be a big help too."

"What's that supposed to mean?" The ranchman cocked his head with a confused expression.

Seeing the look on his face, she reached for his hands. "Jimmy Ray's a good boy and he wants to please you. He loves you and I'm sure he knows you love him, but it's hard on him when you expect so much."

"I expect so much because I know he is capable of so much."

"Have you told him that?"

He thought for a long moment. "No, I suppose I haven't."

"You've bragged on Scott a lot lately. Have you done much bragging on Jimmy Ray?"

He watched her, his mind working. "Scott needs to be bragged on. He's had some problems and needs to be encouraged."

"And Jimmy Ray?"

Ricky made no comment. He retreated to the bed and sat silently, studying the floor, rubbing his bare feet back and forth on the carpet.

She moved to his side and touched his shoulder. "You're a good dad. Jimmy Ray and Jewell love you lots. And I do too." She brushed his black hair from his forehead and cupped his face in her hands. "Jimmy Ray needs some encouragement once in a while too. Don't you think?"

"Yes," he whispered, suddenly feeling guilty but just as quickly feeling frustrated. He gazed up into his wife's eyes. "If he would just get his nose out of those stupid ocean books. What a waste of time. If he spent half as much time learning to be a better cowboy as he did reading those books, he'd be a top hand."

Jessie released his hand then stood to look out the window. It was dark except for a circle of light under a security lamp at the barn. After a long moment, she replied, "Your mom wanted you to be a lawyer. Do you think she was disappointed when you only wanted to hang around the feedlot with Old Jim?"

He stood to look out the window with her. "That's different, I knew all along what I wanted to do. All I ever wanted was to be a cowboy."

She turned to silently gaze into his eyes and once again took his hands in hers. The longer she watched him the more uncomfortable he felt.

"What? Are you saying he wants to be an ocean guy?"

She smiled and reached to lightly brush her knuckles across his cheek. "I'm saying that he needs his dad to be proud of him no matter what he wants to be."

"I am proud of him and I love him."

"I know that. Does he?"

Chapter 7

Mom and Dad,
I'm ready to come home anytime now. I know we
agreed on two weeks but I want out. Please come
get me.
Vicente

***

Vicente sat on a lawn chair in the backyard of
Román's house. It was a pleasant winter day and he was
tired of the bunkhouse. He had been there only a few days
and had written the short letter that morning. He held it in
his hand and tapped the envelope on his knee.

He heard the diesel engine of the truck approaching
on the road to the pasture to the south. When the truck
came into view he was not surprised that it was Román. The
ranchman had asked him to help take salt out to the cows
but he had impolitely refused. He had nothing in common
with the man that was his jailer. The less they were together
the better he liked it.

The truck rolled to a stop under a leafless cottonwood
tree. "Hello, Vicente," called Román as he stepped from the
new Ford truck. "Good to see you out of the bunkhouse. It
can get a little small can't it?"

The teen didn't answer, he only walked to his relative
and passed the envelope. "Can you mail this?" he asked with
undisguised hostility.

"I'd be happy to. It's good to see you writing your

folks. They're good people."

Vicente frowned then turned toward the barn and his room. At the corner of the barn he turned to ask, "What time's supper?"

Román had been watching the young man's retreat. "Six o'clock sharp. Would you mind wearing a shirt and not the wife-beater? Lupita doesn't like it."

Vicente heard but pretended he didn't. Without a word, he shuffled around the corner and into the bunkhouse room. He shook his head then proceeded directly to the bed. He lay down and looked at the ceiling with his hands clasped behind his head. *I'm glad she don't like it,* he thought.

***

At 6:00 o'clock Vicente barged into the kitchen without so much as a knock. Lupita was at the stove. She turned and graced him with a smile. His rude entry and the wife-beater t-shirt he wore in express disobedience hadn't seemed to faze her in the least. Vicente frowned at the lack of reaction then plopped down in the chair at the table.

"Hi, Vicente," she greeted. "I hope you like tacos," she said without a trace of hostility.

He cocked his head and studied her, wondering how she could be so composed even though he was doing everything he could to make her mad. He watched her step toward the living room to call the rest of the family for dinner.

"Hello, Vicente," called Román as he entered to stand next to his wife. The couple's daughters, 13 and 16 also came in to sit at the table. Román helped Lupita bring the food to the table then each took the remaining chairs. The family members held hands for grace but Vicente refused to hold either Lupita's hand on his right or Lexi's hand on his left. The prayer was said and the family crossed themselves then started eating.

Vicente was momentarily taken back to his growing up years. His family had said grace over every meal though

58

they didn't hold hands. At the thought he was instantly jealous that this family had everything going for them. They were a ranch family so they were obviously rich and would never understand what it's like to try to eke out a living, barely getting by. He looked around the table at each of the faces. They were happy, smiling faces and they talked of school and friends and current events. He shook his head angry at his own circumstances. Why couldn't he have been born rich like this family?

They tried to include him in their conversation but he sullenly ate more than his share of the food then rose without any hint of a thank you and walked out the door. Back in the isolation of the bunkhouse, he remembered again his family's situation. They had been a loving family he supposed, but that had all changed when they got word that his brother had been killed.

The longer he thought the madder he became and he vowed again to make it through the rest of his time with his cousin, then he could go home.

***

Román tenderly rubbed Lupita's long hair as the couple lay in their bed. Román was on his back while his wife lay on her side with her head on his shoulder. The full moon beamed brightly into the bedroom and neither could sleep. "Did we make a mistake?"

Román contemplated his wife's question. Before going to bed both had noticed Vicente sitting on the ground leaning back on the bunkhouse throwing rocks from the landscape gravel at a horse trailer parked nearby. There was plenty of light to see the look and posture of hatred.

"I hope not," was his reply. "He's full of bluff and bluster but I think down deep he is a scared boy. Let's give him some more time. He's had it pretty rough, losing his brother the way he did. It may take some time but he'll come around.

She snuggled closer and kissed him on the cheek.

***

At breakfast the next morning Lupita made biscuits and planned to serve them with strawberries and whipped cream on top. The table was set and her husband and girls would be there momentarily. The back door opened. She turned expecting Román but was obviously disappointed when the boy walked in. Vicente gleefully watched her smile turn to a frown. The bigger her frown the bigger his smirk. He sat at the table, reached for a biscuit then dumped half the bowl of strawberries onto his plate. He ate quickly and loudly then, as the rest of the family walked to the kitchen, he stood and with a sneer, wastefully dumped what was left on his plate into the garbage then walked out without a word.

The family silently watched him go. Román stepped closer to the door and glared as the youngster retreated to the bunkhouse. The rancher's jaw muscles were tight and his fists were clenched. Though he prided himself on control, he was mad, madder perhaps than he had ever been. His first instinct was to call Sylvia and have her come immediately to get the unrepentant boy. He had volunteered to help but if Vicente didn't want help what was the use. It was obviously time to change tactics. The decision to smother the boy in love and kindness didn't seem to be working. Maybe what his long lost cousin needed was a firmer hand. He'd have to think about that. He took a deep breath, forcing himself to relax. He turned, to see his wife and daughters studying him, no doubt wondering what his course of action might be. He smiled weakly. "Sorry about that. Let's eat and get you girls to school."

***

The girls had gone to the high school basketball game. Román and Lupita sat at the dinner table, both eyeing the empty chair. It was already past 6:00 and Vicente should have come in for supper but he was late again. The boy just couldn't show any respect. He'd been rude at breakfast, quiet, sullen and angry at lunch and now he was making them wait for dinner. Vicente had been at Román's for only a week and every day had been a challenge. The boy didn't want to be there and he made sure Román knew it at every opportunity. He wouldn't help on the ranch nor would he help around the house. He was foul-mouthed and uncooperative and to top that he had refused to show any consideration for Lupita. Román was reaching the breaking point. Kindness and love weren't working, maybe it was time for some rules. His jaw muscles worked under his cheeks at the aggravation. Finally, he stood, threw the napkin onto his empty plate and started toward the door to have a man-to-man talk with his visitor.

As the door opened, he saw Vicente leisurely approaching on the narrow sidewalk. One hand held his pants and he wore the same wife-beater. Román gritted his teeth as he held the door and stood to the side to allow the boy to enter. Each stood, watching the other, each waiting for the other to speak. Vicente said nothing but the look on his face told all.

Román breathed deeply, using all his restraint before talking. "Vicente, we have to come to some kind of understanding. You can't continue to live here acting the way you've been acting. This is a working ranch and you are expected to work. You're our guest and as such certainly are afforded some leeway but I won't have you treating Lupita like your servant. You'll be fed three squares a day but you're going to have to start working for them." He paused, the anger increasing. Raising his voice, he continued, "No more waiting on you hand and foot. If you expect to be treated like a man you're going to have to start acting like a man. *Comprendes*?

Vicente glared at Román with unconcealed hatred. His own voice raised as the pent-up anger exploded in his chest. "I'm no guest here and we all know it." He looked for the briefest instant at Lupita before focusing again on the rancher. "If you want me to go, fine! Take me to the bus station right now. I hate you, I hate this ranch and I hate this town." He turned and stormed out leaving the frustrated couple, slamming the door hard enough to break one of the panes of decorative glass.

Román shoulders sagged and he rubbed his face with both hands. He walked to his chair, sat and dished the enchiladas onto his plate. He refused to look at his wife. This was one of the first times he had ever lost his temper with a boy and he was embarrassed and ashamed that she had witnessed it. They ate together in strained silence and were almost finished with the meal when they heard the truck leave in a spray of gravel. Román hurriedly ran to the side door and watched helplessly as the truck squealed tires when it hit the main road. He returned to the pegboard in the kitchen that held all the keys to the ranch. The truck keys were gone, his truck had been stolen.

***

Vicente didn't know exactly where he was but he did know he was getting out of New Mexico as fast as he could. He hated being cooped up at his cousin's place and there was no way he was going to work for nothing.

The headlights illuminated what appeared to be a straight road stretching into the distance. He increased his speed then panicked as the painted yellow lines made a turn to the left. He braked quickly, but not quickly enough. He attempted to make the turn but the momentum of the truck caused it to leave the road. It bounced up and over a small embankment then hurtled through the air into the ravine below. Near the bottom it hit a large rock which caused it to roll two times.

Vicente didn't know how long he had been trapped in the truck. It was sitting upright and he rested in the driver's seat. Blood trickled down his face from a broken glass cut and his muscles hurt but the seat belt had done its job. He was bruised and his head hurt but he was alive.

A passer-by with a flashlight carefully picked his way from the pavement through the brush to the bottom of the ravine. "Are you okay?" he asked while shining the flashlight at Vicente.

The bright light caused the driver's head to throb even harder. He moved his limbs and turned his head. Everything moved and nothing seemed broken. "Yeah."

"Good. I've called the cops and they should be here any minute. Are you sure you're all right?"

Vicente frowned at the mention of the cops. That's all he needed, to be arrested for stealing a truck. He nodded his head in answer to the question. Within two minutes he heard the siren from the approaching deputy and shortly after another siren from an ambulance. He was expertly extricated and carried on a gurney to the pavement. Ten minutes later he was being wheeled into the emergency room at the Roswell hospital.

**

Román drove his wife's car to the site of the accident and stood at the side of the road with the Sheriff's deputy. The steadily blinking red and blue lights of the patrol car and the yellow flashing lights of the wrecker cast psychedelic patterns into the shadows. Both men were looking into the ravine at the wrecked four-door Ford pickup. Cables had been connected to the truck and an all's clear signal had been given by one of the tow truck men.

The big truck's motor revved as the winch, groaning and creaking, pulled Román's truck onto the roadside from the ravine below. There was no question that it was a total loss. Román shook his head. The truck was only a few months old and had less than two thousand miles on it.

His thoughts turned to Vicente, who had been driving the truck. He was in the hospital in Roswell with cuts and bruises but nothing life threatening. Román and his wife had visited the boy immediately after the call from the Sheriff's Office. After finding out that Vicente would be all right but would be kept in the hospital for possibly two days, Román took his wife home, then drove to the crash site.

The men watched as the truck was pulled onto the

flatbed of the wrecker. As it drove away, the deputy asked Román to join him in the patrol car to work on the accident report. "Is the driver a relative of yours?"

"Yes. He's the son of my cousin."

"His license is from California."

"Yes. He's here working for me."

"Just guessing his speed, I'd say he was driving at least 70 and couldn't make the turn. Any idea why he would be driving so fast on a narrow, winding back road."

Román knew but wasn't willing to say. "I guess he was just being a stupid kid," answered the rancher dejectedly.

"Well, he's a 'lucky to be alive' stupid kid," remarked the deputy as he shook his head and closed the aluminum case that held the report.

Román exited the squad car with a mumbled "thank you" and a wave then ducked into his wife's car for the drive home. He was at his wit's end. He'd had hard to handle boys before, but until Vicente, they had all started coming around as they saw his genuine concern for them. The one thing that kept him willing to continue was remembering the successes, boys like Carlos, Jake and Scott.

His thoughts turned to Scott. The big football player had been uncooperative at first like so many of the others, but within a few days he discovered he liked Román and the ranching lifestyle.

Román entered the house to see his wife waiting for him. The girls were asleep so the couple sat at the kitchen table. "The truck is a total loss. Vicente's lucky he wasn't killed."

"Did you tell the officer that he stole the truck?"

Román shook his head and reached for his wife's hand. "I'm not giving up yet. Getting him arrested for stealing the truck would serve no good purpose. He'll come around. Maybe this wreck will wake him up."

The wife pursed her lips and he could see by the look on her face that she didn't believe him. He reached to tenderly brush her long, dark hair from her face. "Do you remember Carlos, Scott, Simon and Rafael? They all came around. Let's give Vicente some more time. Sooner or later, he'll realize what his life can be like."

She rewarded him with a tender smile. "You are so patient and kind."

He stood and pulled her to her feet. "Ah, I owe that to you and the unwavering support you give. Will it be okay with you to let him stay a little longer?"

"*Si, Patrón*," she replied, using the title he requested of the boys. She hugged him lovingly.

***

Jessie and Jewell had been fixing breakfast when they were interrupted by the ringing of the phone in the living room. The boys were out at the barn making final preparations for the roundup that was scheduled to start the next day. She stepped to the back porch. "Ricky, it's Román on the phone. He wants to talk to you and Scott."

The big teenager held the door for Ricky and Jimmy Ray. When all three were in the house, Ricky picked up the handset. "Hello, Friend Román."

"Hello, Ricky."

He sounded tired. The rancher was immediately concerned. "Are you okay, Román?"

"I'm fine. I just wanted to call and see how Scott was getting along."

"He's doing great. Here, I'll let you talk to him." He handed the phone to the muscular young man."

"Hello, *Patrón*." He pronounced it with the accent on the first syllable and an ah instead of an o sound at the end. Ricky couldn't speak much Spanish but he still cringed.

"Hi, Scott. I wanted to call to see how you were doing there with my good friend Ricky."

"Very well. We start roundup tomorrow and I'm excited to be able to help."

"Good for you. Have there been any...temptations?"

Scott chuckled. "No, sir. We're 18 miles from a town that has fewer people than my high school and I'm loving it."

"I'm proud of you," said Román as he thought to himself, *Sounds like a place Vicente needs to be.*

Scott placed the handset on the phone table, then walked into the kitchen. "He wants to talk to you, *Patrón.*"

Ricky listened as he held the phone to his ear. "I just wanted to visit for a minute. I sure appreciate you taking Scott in. That's been a big help."

"It's been our pleasure. How are things working out with the new boy you have there?"

There was a pause on the phone. Finally, Román answered in a quiet voice, "Not quite as well as I'd hoped." He then told of the wrecked truck and Vicente's hospital stay. "But enough of that. I didn't call to complain. I'm just glad that things are working out so well with Scott." He chuckled as he recounted to Ricky what Scott had told him about being so far away from any temptations.

Ricky thought for the slightest moment. He didn't know the reason and for months after he wondered why he volunteered. "If you think it would help, bring the new boy here. There's not much he can do to get in trouble. And maybe having someone like Scott might help him get his head on straight."

"I couldn't ask you to do that."

"Nonsense. If you think it would do him any good, bring him on."

There was a longer pause on the phone. Finally, Román said, "He'll get out of the hospital probably tomorrow. He'll be too sore to move for another week. How about both of us come and spend a few days with you then?"

"Looking forward to it. We'll be finished with roundup by then and I've got a grant from the Conservation Service to build three miles of cross fence. I could use the help."

Chapter 8

Jessie started breakfast at 4:00 while Ricky went out to grain the horses. By 5:00, though it was still dark and cold, the men had the horses caught and were saddling them at the barn. Trucks and trailers of neighbors and friends started arriving and horses were unloaded. By dawn, 9 hands were mounted and on their way at a half trot to one of the big pastures where half of the cows were. Jimmy Ray was the youngest of the group. The oldest was Ricky's good friend and neighbor, Bob Laramore, at 78, a recently retired Texas state senator.

"I hope none of you boys get bucked off on a cool morning like this," commented Ricky. The group laughed but really got engaged as the buckskin colt Ricky was riding spooked at a rabbit jumping out from a bush. The ranch owner had just enough of a warning that he was able to stay with the hard bucking three-year-old.

Ricky had only recently started the big buckskin and he was coming along nicely. When he had caught the colt early that morning, he stopped to give Pardner a rub on his forehead under the glow of the security light in the pre-dawn darkness. He wasn't riding him on this morning because the horse was getting older. Roundups were for younger, stronger horses. The thought made the young rancher melancholy. "Time's are changing aren't they?" he commented as he rubbed the big horse's ears before leading his mount for the day out of the horse corral and over to the barn.

By two that afternoon the cattle were all in the big set of working corrals next to the house. The late winter day was comfortably warm and the sun was shining brightly. The gather of the first pasture had gone well and they were ahead of schedule. It only took thirty minutes to have the calves branded then another thirty minutes sorting out the older cows to sell and the crew was finished for the day. One more day gathering the cows in the adjoining pasture would have the roundup finished for the spring except for going back to brand any new calves in the coming weeks.

As the cowboys made their way toward the house after tying their horses to the fence, Ricky stood to the side. Behind him he could hear the cows bawling if they had not yet found their calves. Toward the house, he could see his expansive driveway full of cars and trucks. The wives and kids of the friends and neighbors had come for the pot luck meal. It had become a tradition looked forward to by all. He smiled contentedly at the sight. *Life is good!* he thought to himself.

***

Román and his wife entered the Roswell hospital and walked directly to Vicente's room. Any hopes that he had learned a lesson and might come around evaporated immediately as they entered. The television high on the wall blared pounding rap music and Vicente completely ignored them as they placed a set of clean clothes on the bed.

"The doc said you could come home," said Román. "We brought you these clothes from your suitcase in the bunkhouse. The one's you were wearing the other night are dirty and bloody."

"Are you taking me to my home or back to my stall in the barn?" He turned to face them with a venomous expression.

Román's jaw muscles could be seen working under the skin. "We'll go home to our place. If you'd like, you can hang out on the living room couch until you feel better."

"Yeah. Whatever."

Román took his wife's hand. "We'll wait for you in the lobby. Come on up when you finish dressing." The couple turned to walk out the door. After two steps in the hall, Román stopped and reentered the room. "We're glad you weren't seriously injured."

"Yeah, I bet you are," said the teen contemptuously.

Vicente waited until they left, then delayed another ten minutes just to show them they couldn't boss him around. Finally, he slowly rolled out of the hospital bed. He was sore and it hurt to move. He put on his shirt and pants but couldn't bend over far enough to pull on his socks. He slipped into the tennis shoes and stuffed the rolled up pair of socks in his pocket. He hadn't talked to his mom or dad since being left in Roswell but he had counted the days. The two weeks of the agreement were coming to an end. At the start, it seemed so far in the future that he wondered if the day would ever arrive. Now he was just a few days away but a gnawing suspicion that the two weeks would be extended had him worried. He left the letter addressed to his parents on the food tray with two quarters for postage. He hoped the nurse would mail it for him.

> Mom and Dad,
>
> I'm really ready to come home. I hate it here.
>
> Vicente

"Just a few more days," he mumbled as he left the room.

Slowly, he made his way to the lobby. Román and his wife stood as he approached. He ignored them again, shuffling toward the front doors. When he was outside, he noticed that it had rained. The wind across the wet ground was bitter and cold. He turned and noticed for the first time that both Román and his wife had jackets. "What? No jacket for me?" he asked with his palms up.

"If you like, you can wait inside while I bring the truck around."

Without a word, the ungrateful teenager returned to

the warmth of the hospital lobby. He watched out the window as the couple walked to a brand-new four-door Ford pickup. They drove to the hospital entrance. As Vicente watched, his hatred grew. *How is it that other people can just go and buy things? A brand-new truck just like that. Why am I the only one who has to struggle all the time? It's so easy for them.*

As the truck stopped, he exited the hospital and pulled himself into the back seat of the truck. It hurt but he gritted his teeth and didn't show it. Once inside, he slammed the door as hard as he could just to make them mad, then sat with arms folded. "Home, James."

Román smiled and Vicente noticed the tender look he gave his wife. They had obviously been talking and had decided to return to the love and kindness option. Fine with me, thought the youngster in the back seat. I can outlast them.

They drove to the garage. "Come on in the house," invited the rancher. "You have a package from your folks. It's on the kitchen table."

Vicente strolled through the garage door, down the short hall to the kitchen, anxious to see what his parents might have sent. He noticed the cardboard square that had been taped over the broken pane and felt a small stirring of regret. He quickly pushed that feeling to the side, vowing to make it through this confinement till he could go home. He held the large, manila envelope and looked over his shoulder to see if anyone was watching. No one was. He unlocked the back door and walked out to the bunkhouse.

At the small desk he slid his finger under the flap which lifted easily. He dumped the contents onto the scarred wood of the desktop. The first thing he saw was a letter with his mom's handwriting. He read quickly.

Dearest Vicente,

Your father and I miss you so much but are glad you are out of danger. We are lonely here but healthy and all is well. I wanted to send you this picture of Antonio and the letters he wrote to you while he was in Iraq. I miss him so much that I can hardly stand it but at least we have his picture and letters to remember him. He loved you and we love you too.

We hope you and Román are getting along well. He is a good man and you can learn a lot from him. Take care and we will see you soon.

Love you,

Mom

Slowly, he turned the cardboard backed eight by ten-inch photograph over. Antonio stared out handsomely with a serious expression, the white dress issue cap in stark contrast to the painstakingly pressed blue Marine uniform, the American flag at his side brightly showing the red and white stripes under the blue field with silver stars.

Vicente had the picture memorized. He had stared at it for hours on end while his brother was away. He had revered Antonio. His older brother had been big and strong, handsome and smart. It was a proud day in the house when he enlisted and Vicente at the time had decided to join the Marines as soon as he was old enough.

He closed his eyes as he remembered the last time Antonio had been home on a two-day-pass before being shipped out. They had eaten dinner as a family, then sat on the back porch in the summer breeze enjoying each other's company. The mother had instructed several times that he should be careful to which the proud Marine flippantly responded, "You don't have to worry about me. I'll be fine."

But he wasn't fine. Two months into his tour a group of seemingly innocuous civilians approached the platoon. From the corner of his eye he noticed a man to the side pulling a gun from his robes. Antonio sprang into action but was too late. The automatic weapon was pointed in his direction and he was hit hard with the first burst along with three fellow Marines. Antonio brought his own gun to bear and silenced the threat but his own wounds were too severe.

Vicente thought of the day the immaculately uniformed Marines brought the news and he remembered their somber expressions and guessed their thoughts of the moment of a fine young man taken in the prime of his life by a senseless act in a country that didn't want him there. Vicente remembered the relatives stopping by with platitudes but no one could know of the loss, the fear and even the hate one feels at such a devastating loss. He groaned at the recollection. He viciously slapped the light switch then lay on the bed in the dark.

***

The second day of the roundup didn't start out as smoothly as the first. Early that morning, Ricky noticed that the big palomino Scott had been riding came to eat the grain with a pronounced limp.

He caught the horse and led him slowly out of the pen to the hitching rail at the barn directly under the security light. Ricky could now see that the horse was in a lot of pain. He ran his hand down the horse's right front leg. The horse flinched and Ricky felt a number of cactus thorns protruding from just above the hair line.

"Looks like you found a cholla cactus," he commented to the horse. Talking to his horses was a habit he didn't feel the least bit self-conscious about.

Leaving the horse until he could see better, Ricky realized he was now one horse short. As he made his way to the breakfast table where Jessie had just served breakfast to Scott and Jimmy Ray, he told them about the crippled horse and reminded them to try to keep their horses out of the cactus.

He then turned to his son. "Jimmy Ray, what if Scott rides Old Dunny today and you ride Pardner?"

Jesse and Jimmy Ray quickly reacted. No one other than Ricky ever rode Pardner.

"I guess so," answered the boy. He had grown up with the stories of how hard the horse bucked. "He won't buck me off will he?"

His dad smiled. "Not if you don't touch his neck while you're getting off."

Jimmy Ray sat silently in his own little world. Ricky watched Jessie observing their son and he knew that she knew what he was thinking. A slow smile came across the boy's face. His dad was letting him ride Pardner! That was probably the highest compliment he had ever received. He looked at his mother and she saw his smile. She watched as he attacked his biscuits and gravy with enthusiasm.

Jessie turned to Ricky. He nodded and winked. Her smile was as wide as Ricky had ever seen it.

As the cowboys left the house at a half trot on the way to the pasture, Jimmy Ray rode alongside his dad for the first time in a long time.

During the roundup, Ricky noticed his son doing more than he had ever done in the past. He was riding Pardner and making a top hand. When the cattle were all in the corral, the cowboys gathered at the big water trough to let their horses drink. Jimmy Ray rode beside his dad and let the long, split reins dangle loosely so Pardner could drink his fill. The horse put his nose in the water half way to his eyes and splashed with a shake of his head. Then he drank.

"You're making a good hand today, Son. Is Old Pardner treating you right?"

"Yes, sir. He doesn't act like he's getting old. He wants to be where the action is." Jimmy Ray leaned back and patted the big horse on the hip.

Ricky looked at his son with pride. "He's sure taken care of me and I'm glad he's taking care of you now too."

Chapter 9

Sunday morning, Ricky, Scott and Jimmy Ray saddled horses to ride the fence lines of the two pastures to make sure there were no cows trying to find their way through looking for ways back into the pasture they had been in up until the roundup. Jimmy Ray was the first one out to the horse pen. Ricky was surprised when he left the house to catch his colt to see his son already mounted and ready to ride. But he wasn't on Dunny, he sat relaxed and smiling on Pardner.

"Looking good, Son," commented the dad on his way past. The youngster's smile broadened.

***

Monday morning arrived, the roundup was finished and things were back to normal at the ranch house. Jimmy Ray and Jewell caught the bus at 6:30 for school, Ricky and Scott fed the calves in the weaning pen then drove the truck to check on a windmill that had been making a squealing sound the last time they had ridden by.

Ricky stood on the platform 40 feet above the ground at the top of the windmill. He hated heights and held tightly to a waist-high, solid part of the windmill. He had the top cover off and was studying the gears. "I think all it needs is some oil," he hollered down to Scott who stood shielding his eyes from the glaring sun as he watched from below.

The big youngster turned to retrieve a gallon jug and a

rope from the back of the truck. He threw the coiled rope toward the rancher. Ricky reached for it but in reaching lost his balance and his handhold. He grasped frantically for anything to keep him from falling but the only thing he grabbed was the top cover of the gearbox that sat unattached on the platform. It sailed through the air and dropped to the ground below. Ricky's arms flailed as he tried to regain his balance but it was no use. In slow motion, he started to fall but in falling he was able to kick free and like a cat, turned in midair to grab the outside board on the platform. He hung there desperately, swinging with dangling legs. His hands gripped tightly to the slick, painted board, but to his horror he could feel them slipping.

In that instant, he knew that a fall from this height would kill him for sure. In desperation he gripped tighter but his fingers ever so slowly slipped toward the edge and a certain fall. He flailed his legs trying to find something, anything to hold his weight but they dangled and kicked thin air. He searched to the side to see if perhaps he could grab one of the tower braces but couldn't find anything close enough to reach. He looked up to see his fingers almost to the end of the platform.

In resigned terror, he watched as his fingers slipped at last away from the boards and he screamed as he fell. His screaming continued long after he should have reached the ground. It was only then that he felt the viselike grip around his midsection. Turning his head he saw Scott, one hand on the tower ladder and one arm holding him in midair.

Ricky turned to wrap his arms tightly around the boy's neck. His breathing was rapid, panting almost like a dog because of the absolute terror he had experienced.

"*Patrón*, I can't breathe," choked Scott.

It took seconds for Ricky to realize what the boy had said and more seconds until the rancher relinquished the iron-hard grip on the muscular neck.

Ricky found the rungs of the ladder with his feet then slowly and with one arm firmly attached to Scott's neck, he reached with his other hand to take his own position on the ladder. Only after he had two feet and one hand securely planted did he release his grip on Scott's neck. The boy took two quick steps up to allow his boss complete access to the rungs.

Ricky held tightly, still too afraid and shaken to move. He shuddered uncontrollably and his breath continued in short gasps. At length he slowly climbed down the ladder then sat heavily on the ground with his head in his hands. His breathing was heavy as though he had run a race. Scott joined him on the ground.

"I'm sorry, *Patrón*," apologized the big boy. "I should have thrown the rope better."

Ricky shook his head and didn't answer for a full minute. He had been shaken to the very core. Finally, he looked up at the teen. "It wasn't your fault. My hand slipped as I leaned out. If you hadn't grabbed me I'd have fallen for sure." He looked up at the tower and shuddered at the thought.

They sat on the ground for a long time. Ricky didn't speak so Scott was quiet also. After a time the rancher leaned to the football player and rested his hand on his shoulder. Squeezing gently he said, "Thank you, Scott. Thank you."

***

Tuesday was spent gathering fencing materials. The old 1950 something flatbed fencing truck was gassed up and ready to go. A bed was made up for Román in the guest bedroom in the house and one was made for Vicente in the bunkhouse. They arrived just after sundown. The family and Scott were just finishing supper. They went out to greet the newcomers.

Their guests got out of the truck in less than a good mood. The trip had been a long one simply because Vicente had complained the whole way. "I'm supposed to be heading home. My folks promised only two weeks," he had reminded over and over.

"Just a few days here with Ricky. You'll like him."

"Yeah, I'm sure I will," countered the young man sarcastically.

At the ranch while getting out of the truck Román reminded Vicente, "We're guests here. Please act like it." He reached back into the truck and took his silver, felt cowboy hat and placed it carefully on his head.

"Hello, Román." Ricky pumped the smaller man's hand vigorously.

"*Hola, Patrón*," greeted Scott.

Román made the rounds, then turned to Vicente who had been standing to the side in baggy pants, a white wife-beater t-shirt, two ear studs and an Oakland Raiders ball cap pulled down low. "I'd like to introduce Vicente." Then gesturing toward Jimmy Ray, he said, "This is Jimmy Ray."

"Hello, *muchacho*," said Vicente with obvious disdain.

"This is Scott."

Vicente sneered at the massive teenager's size, "Hello, *Flaco*."

Román gritted his teeth. "This is my good friend Ricky."

"Hello, *Putrón*."

Ricky knew enough Spanish to know that all three had been insulted and he, worst of all because of the play on the word. Before he or Román could react, Scott stepped in front of the thin, 5'8" teenager. Obviously, he understood some Spanish also. Looking down, trembling with rage but exhibiting amazing control, he quietly said, "Friend, you can insult me all you want but when you insult my friends, I'll put a stop to it—and don't make the mistake of thinking I won't."

The two glared at one another for a few seconds until Vicente stepped back and shrugged his shoulders, replying, "Whatever."

Ricky spoke to break the tension. "Have you eaten? We've got plenty."

"We're fine," replied Román. "We stopped on the road

and got a bite to eat."

"Well, come on in the house and relax from the trip. The group started inside. Vicente pushed toward the front but Scott held his arm out to prevent the new teenager from entering before Ricky and Román. Vicente tried to push the arm away but it was immovable. Scott stood like an oak tree. When the others were in the house, Scott stepped back, allowing the new teen to enter as he followed.

Inside the living room, the family and visitors sat. Vicente had chosen a hard-backed chair as far away from the others as possible. Scott pulled an empty recliner to sit next to him. Ricky introduced Jessie and Jewell but Scott was so close to Vicente that he dared not make any disparaging comment. He looked at them with a sneer but kept his mouth shut.

Scott leaned close to Vicente's ear and whispered, "Take your hat off. We're in the house."

Vicente tried to scoot his chair away but an iron grip held it in place. He stole a glance at the big football player, then slowly reached up to remove his hat.

Scott smiled. He leaned back and folded his arms.

Román, Jessie and Ricky spent the next hour visiting and telling stories. They occasionally looked at Vicente, noticing that he sat there quietly, hat in hand. Román was happily impressed. Shortly, noticing Jewell nodding off to sleep, he said, "I think we had best get to bed if you're expecting any fence to get built tomorrow. If you'll just show us where to go, we'll get settled in for the night."

Ricky nodded happily. "You'll stay in the guest bedroom in the house." Then, turning to the massive teen, he asked, "Scott, would you mind helping Vicente get settled in the bunkhouse?"

"It'll be my pleasure, *Patrón.*" He stood at the side of Vicente's chair and eyed the newcomer, waiting for him to stand. All he got was a defiant stare and an obscene gesture from Vicente's right hand while the left held the hat to keep anyone else from seeing it.

Scott reached down and effortlessly lifted the chair, spilling Vicente to the floor in the process. "I'm sorry. Let me help you up," he said in an uncharacteristically mocking voice. He grabbed the thin boy's left elbow and lifted him to his feet.

Vicente reared back and swung a hard right fist at Scott's jaw. The big teen was too quick. He caught the fist with his free hand, stopping it six inches from his face. He held an elbow in one hand and a fist in the other as he faced Jimmy Ray. "It seems as though he dropped his hat. If you would be so kind as to pick it up, I'm sure he would appreciate it. Won't you Vicente?"

Scott squeezed both hands tighter, the vise-like pressure hurting the boy. His knees had gone weak but he was being held up by the pressure on his arm. "Yes," he choked.

Still holding his elbow, Scott released the hand so Vicente could take his hat. He led the way out the door and on to the bunkhouse with the slightly older but much smaller teen's elbow held tightly. When they were gone, Román glanced at Ricky. "I hope they don't hurt each other."

***

Scott and Vicente walked into the house for breakfast. Everyone else was already seated at the table and looked up as the two teens entered through the side door. Scott nodded at Ricky and Román, then, sliding his cowboy hat under the chair, took his customary seat next to Jewell. Vicente stood, waiting and watching with dark sunglasses covering his face under his Raiders cap.

"Your hat can go under your chair," said Scott conversationally as he turned to see the smaller teen standing with his hat still on his head. Vicente quickly removed his hat.

"You can sit here," instructed Jessie, pulling an empty chair from the table.

Vicente sat without a word then bent to place his hat

under his chair. Román noticed Scott's smile as he reached for the pan of biscuits.

***

Two ranch owners rode in a ranch truck and two teenagers rode in an old 50's something fencing truck to the middle of the ranch. They unloaded shovels and tamping bars to dig post holes to set a corner brace. Scott, Ricky and Román each took a turn with the heavy bar, breaking up the ground so the loose dirt could be shoveled out. When Román finished, he noticed Scott standing very close to Vicente. The big youngster nodded in the smaller teen's direction. Román tried to hide his smile but couldn't. He passed the bar to his distant cousin who took it with a look of aggravation toward the football player. After only going through the motions with three effortless hits, he passed the bar to Ricky, then stood on the other side of the hole. Scott joined him there.

"Get away from me. What are you, gay or something?" Vicente then reached up, slapped his tormentor then sprinted away.

It happened so quickly there was no time to react. The two older cowboys watched in amazement as Vicente ran, one hand holding his pants up, with Scott hot on his heels. The smaller boy was quicker and the first 30 yards saw him in the lead, but as the distance grew, his stamina was exhausted and the soreness from the wreck was evident. Try as he might, he couldn't outrun Scott, who overtook the thin teen and tackled him in a sand wash out of sight from their mentors.

The two older men ran to the wash to save a life. When they got there they found Scott sitting on Vicente's chest. The smaller boy's arms were pinned under the bigger boy's knees. Vicente could only thrash his head and try to kick with his feet but nothing he did had the least effect on Scott.

Román stopped Ricky at the bank of the wash, motioning for him to be quiet. Vicente was not in physical danger but he was obviously getting an earful, although the cowboys on the bank couldn't hear what was being said. Román tapped Ricky on the shoulder, signaling for him to retreat. When they were out of earshot, he said, "Let's jog on back and not let them know we saw. I think Scott is handling Vicente pretty well. This may be just what he needs."

They picked up the bar and shovel and were hard at work at the post hole, seemingly unaware of the absence of the youths as they returned ten minutes later with Vicente leading and Scott following closely. When it was Vicente's turn with the bar, he stepped to the hole and used the bar like it was meant to be used. He stepped back and passed the bar to Scott, noticing but ignoring a nod of recognition from the bigger teen.

Ricky stepped to his truck and rummaged around in the back for a bit. He returned in two minutes with a length of soft rope which he held for Vicente. The teen studied the rope for several seconds with obvious confusion.

"Use it as a belt to hold your pants up," volunteered the young rancher.

Vicente made a face and shook his head but as he noticed them watching him he jerked the rope out of Ricky's hand and cussed while feeding it through the loops. He tied the front so loosely that it did nothing to hold his pants up but within an hour Ricky noticed that he had secretly tightened it sufficient to hold his pants in place.

The men made good progress. By lunch they had set the posts and built four corners and three in-line braces for fence stretching. Román was proud of Vicente. He had worked alongside the rest with no complaint, but it was obvious he was all done in. He wasn't accustomed to hard physical labor. He took his sandwiches and soda to a shady spot under a cedar tree. He wolfed down his lunch then lay on the ground and was asleep in less than a minute.

At 5:00 that afternoon, the end of a good day's work, the fencing crew was finished for the day and ready to head to the house. While loading the truck, Scott noticed Vicente looking to the west. He followed the gaze and saw a rider on a black horse loping toward them.

"*Patrón.*"

Ricky turned to see the big teen pointing with a jerk of his head. He saw right away that it was Jimmy Ray on Pardner, coming toward them in a smooth, ground covering lope. Jimmy Ray was riding well and Ricky decided he looked mighty good sitting on the black horse, but the sudden appearance was unsettling.

"Is anything wrong?" Ricky asked as Jimmy Ray rode close.

"No, sir. I got off the bus and wanted to check on y'all and Pardner looked like he wanted to be ridden."

"You kind of like him don't you?"

Jimmy Ray nodded.

"Do you know that since I've owned him, you and I are the only ones to ride him and not get bucked off?"

The youngster grinned. "Yes, sir."

The dad grinned back. "Well, we were just heading to the house. Will you do me a favor?"

"Yes, sir."

"Will you jog over to the Lane mill and check the water level of the tank there. Then you can ride down the ridge line and probably beat us back home."

A grin and a nod was the answer. Jimmy Ray turned his mount to the north and loped into the distance with Ricky watching thoughtfully.

"I didn't think anyone but you ever rode that black horse." Román leaned on the bed of the ranch truck enjoying the proud look of a father for his son.

"He started riding him last week. I may never get him back."

***

Vicente went straight to bed after a light dinner. Scott went to the bunkhouse an hour later to read before turning in for the night. He noticed a folded note on his pillow. He started to read. "*Flaco*, you need to chill." As he unfolded the note to read further, a medium-sized, white pill fell from the note and bounced on the bedspread.

Scott recognized it immediately and at the recognition his whole body tensed. He had told himself many times that he was over the cravings but seeing the pill made his breath rate increase and his fingers itch. He stared and swallowed hard. A wave of craving washed up over his shoulders and around to his chest. He wanted it so badly. He glanced to the other side of the room noticing Vicente asleep on his bed. *It's only one. No one will know. What harm could it do?*

Chapter 10

Scott reached for the pill. He held it in his palm, slowly rolling it with the fingers of his other hand. The craving was severe, almost more than he could handle until he noticed a small photograph in a frame on a lamp stand next to his bed. It was a picture of his mother.

He looked from the photograph to the pill in his hand, and back again. His mom loved him and he loved her. Of all the mental anguish he had gone through because of his drug problem, the most severe was the knowledge that he had hurt her, that she was disappointed in him.

He studied the pill in his hand, his breathing slowing, his resolve increasing. After four quick steps to the bathroom he threw the pill into the toilet and pushed the handle. He took a deep breath as he watched the pill swirl for a short time then disappear.

He sat on his bed, his big body shaking uncontrollably. The night was cold, but he put on his jacket and walked into the darkness toward the horse pen. He climbed up to sit on the top rail. Listening to the horses eat was therapeutic, it calmed him. Slowly, his breathing returned to normal. The craving had diminished but he admitted to himself that it was still there. Then, with a rush of emotion, he realized what he had done. He was too shaken to smile, but knowing that he had withstood the temptation gave him a feeling of wellbeing, of confidence. *I really can do this.*

***

It was 5:30 the next morning. "Hey! What do you think you're doing?" screamed Vicente. He had been awakened by the noise at his bedside and sat up to see Scott dumping his suitcase.

"Finding these." The big teen held up a vial half-full of the medium-sized white pills.

"Dude, that's all I have. They have to last me till I go home. I shared one but you can't have the whole bottle."

"Wanna bet?" Scott strode to the bathroom and emptied the entire vial into the toilet. Vicente, in his underwear, had followed him. He shrieked as he watched the pills splash into the water and yelled, "Noooo!" as the big teen pushed the handle.

He jumped on the big boy's back, legs locking around the waist and a choking grip at the throat. He held tightly and squeezed, his rage adding strength.

Scott grasped the arm around his neck to escape but the grip was too tight. He followed the arm with his fingers toward Vicente's hand and was able to pull a finger from the fist. He bent the finger back, causing the smaller teen to scream at the pain and relax his grip. Scott was able to pull the arm over his head and duck out of the choke hold. He turned, gasping for breath to see a panicked look on Vicente's face.

The older of the teens tried to escape but Scott's grip on his arm was too tight. A hard jerk on the arm brought Vicente into a bear hug. He was lifted off the floor by the big football player, the pressure was extreme. His ribs felt like they would be crushed any second. He was carried away from the bathroom and dropped to the floor on his back. He sucked a lungful of air but it was quickly expelled as Scott sat on his chest, pinning his arms just as he had the day before.

Vicente couldn't move, he could barely breathe. He tried to spit in his tormentor's face but couldn't get enough breath so the spittle landed on his own cheek. Finally, he lay still, waiting for the inevitable punch in the face, but it never came.

Scott folded his arms on his chest catching his own breath. Finally, he said, "You just don't get it do you?"

Vicente merely stared at the slightly younger boy, the hatred plain on his face.

"I don't want to hurt you, but I will if you keep giving me reasons. It took me a while to wake up. One of these days you'll wake up too. Until then, I suggest you go along to get along."

Scott pushed to his feet and deliberately turned his back. Vicente rolled to a kneeling position, then stood, wiped his face and stepped to his bed. He climbed in and pulled the blankets over his head.

Scott entered the side door of the house and took his customary chair at the breakfast table. Everyone else was already seated. When the question about Vicente was asked by Román, the massive youth simply shrugged and answered, "Still in bed."

Román frowned, then excused himself and left the house. He knocked and waited for an answer before entering. When no answer came, he opened the door to step through. He saw the boy lying on the bed, completely covered. "Vicente? Vicente, you need to come to the house for breakfast. You can't work with no fuel."

"I'm sick. I can't work today," came the muffled answer.

"I'm sorry to hear that. Come on and get something to eat. That'll make you feel better."

"I told you I'm sick. Maybe I can work tomorrow," he said, feigning sincerity, no doubt hoping that a contrite show of willingness on his part would appease his second cousin.

"Very well. Is there anything I can do to help you feel better?"

"No. I just need to rest."

By the time Román got back in the house, everyone else had finished eating. Jimmy Ray and Jewell were bundled up against the cool breeze, walking to the bus and Ricky and Scott were making last preparations for another day of fence work. He noticed Jessie cleaning the table and counters from breakfast and knew he didn't want her at the ranch alone with Vicente. He frowned, then walked out to see Ricky.

"Vicente is sick and won't be able to go out with us today. Maybe I'd better stay around the house. I don't want him here alone with Jessie."

Ricky leaned on the hood of the truck tracing patterns in the dust that had collected there. "It'll sure make a long day for you." He then brightened with an idea. "Jessie's been needing to go to San Angelo to do some shopping. What if she did that and we made it a half day on the fence? Maybe by noon he'll feel better."

Román looked over the bed of the truck to the bunkhouse. "I suppose that would work. You'll want to make sure none of the vehicles have keys in them. I'm not sure he would still be here at noon if he could get in a truck and drive away."

Ricky counted the vehicles on his fingers as he explained, "We'll have my truck and the fencing truck, Jessie will have her truck and the jeep is broke down and hasn't run for years. If you keep your keys he'll have nothing to drive. Of course, he could saddle a horse but my guess is that he won't go that route."

Román was warming to the idea. "Is there anything he can do here to get himself into trouble?"

"Nah. As tired as he was yesterday, he'll probably sleep all day anyway. I'll go tell Jessie to get the kids before they get on the bus. She can take them to school on her way to town."

"Okay then. Let's go stretch some wire."

***

Vicente got out of bed at 10:00 o'clock. He was hungry

so he dressed quickly and made a bee-line for the house. When he got there the door was locked. He bent and holding a hand against the glare peeked inside the decorative, triangle glass panes built into the door. Seeing no one he stepped back looking around wondering where everyone was. He started working his way to each side of the house and tried the doors, all were locked. He stood back, realizing for the first time that he was at the ranch house completely alone.

This was the first time he had been alone since his parents had more or less kidnapped him and forced him to go to Román's house in Roswell. He hated Román and Ricky. He hated Roswell and he hated it here even more. And most of all he hated the big loser Scott, and he couldn't shake the feeling that Román was going to leave him in this God forsaken place. *I'm outta here*, he decided. *There has to be a car or truck here somewhere that I could use to get away.*

He ran to the garage. Román's truck was there so he quickly tried the doors. All locked. He kicked the tire and swore, thinking that if he just had some of the tools and devices his gang buddies had he could be in the truck on his way. He'd watched some of them steal a locked car in less than 30 seconds. He swore again.

He remembered seeing a yellow jeep in the barn so he ran to see if it was still there. It was and it had the key in the ignition! He grinned, ready to get away. He jumped into the driver's seat, pushed in the clutch and turned the key. Nothing. He slapped the steering wheel in disgust.

More deliberate now, he searched every direction for a drivable vehicle but his search was fruitless. *There has to be a way for me to get away from here.* He heard one of the horses whinny in the horse pen but just as suddenly as the thought came to him, he dismissed it. *I can't ride and it would take too long.*

He dejectedly sat in a swing on the porch, mad that he was there. A devious plan to get away started taking shape.

He personally hadn't done anything like it before, but he remembered one of his gang buddies had told him how to start a fire and make it look like an accident. The plan became more focused. *If there's nowhere for anyone to live, Román will have to take me back to Roswell. I'll be able to get away from there.*

Vicente tried the windows to the house. The one to the little girl's bedroom slid open. In two seconds he was inside. He searched drawers in the kitchen. When he found the tool drawer he pulled out a screwdriver and a utility knife. While standing on the table he removed the cover and then the fixture from the dining room light. Just as he suspected, the wires leading from the ceiling were solid but the light fixture wires were stranded.

It took less than a minute to strip back the plastic covering. He then bent and cut all but one of the thin strands of copper wire. He replaced the wire nut connector and left the light hanging while he rushed to the laundry room. He pulled the lint catcher from the electric dryer and ran back to the kitchen with a handful of lint which he wrapped around the naked strands. When the light was turned on and electricity flowed, those two strands would become increasingly hot. If all went as planned, the lint would ignite and a fire would start in the ceiling and no one would be able to blame him. At least that is what his gang buddy had claimed.

He turned the switch, the light came on. Satisfied with his work, he reattached the light fixture, replaced the tools and cleaned any evidence of his actions before exiting through the window and hurrying back to the bunkhouse.

Ricky, Román and Scott returned at noon and made themselves sandwiches for lunch. Scott was sent to the bunkhouse to ask Vicente if he would like to join them. The thin teen was starving, though he did his best to act otherwise.

After lunch, Román asked, "Do you feel good enough to help us this afternoon? We have some fence to build."

Vicente quickly realized that when the fire started, the farther away he was from the house, the better. "I'll go with you."

Chapter 11

Román tied one end of the barbed wire on to the wooden crosstie that made up the back corner of the brace. Scott ran one of the six-foot tamping bars through the center hole of the wire roll. He turned to Vicente. "Grab that end and let's go."

"Go where?"

"A quarter mile to the next brace." He pointed with a nod of his head.

Vicente frowned. "Are you kidding me? I ain't no mule."

"Neither am I," answered Scott. "This is man's work. I guess you just aren't man enough to do it."

"Oh, yeah? I could work you under the table any time I wanted."

"There's no doubt that your mouth works good. How about the rest of you?"

Vicente recognized the dare and his pride would not let him turn it down. He stepped quickly to his end of the bar and picked it up. "See if you can keep up," he challenged.

The teens, one on each end of the bar started walking with the roll of wire spinning as it unrolled. Up and down, they followed the terrain in as straight a line as possible to the next set of posts. Vicente was anxious to get to the end and though the wire roll should have gotten lighter as more and more of the fence line was left behind, it seemed as heavy toward the end as at the start. *I'm really out of shape,* he inwardly confessed. "Let's stop and rest for a sec."

"But we're only 40 yards from the end. You can see *Patrón* Ricky waiting for us."

It was no use. The thin teenager stopped, dropped his end of the bar and stood with his hands on his knees, breathing hard.

After three minutes, Scott asked, "Are you ready to finish this roll?"

Without a word, only a sour look toward the other teen, Vicente took his end of the bar and together they unrolled the wire the final 40 yards. The thin teen immediately sat on the ground and watched as Ricky cut the wire from the nearly depleted roll and set the stretching tool.

"Scott, you start taking some clicks on the come-along while I walk back and flip the wire to make sure it's in a straight line. I'll tell you when to stop once it gets tight enough."

Scott waited at the come-along as the boss walked back along the strand of wire.

"Okay, start stretching." Then a short time later, "That's good."

Scott watched his companion. "You ready to go back?"

"Back?"

"Back to the truck. We need to drive the steel posts now."

Vicente shrugged his shoulders. He was exhausted. His arms ached, his feet hurt and to make matters worse, his pants were ripped. He admitted that he liked the idea of driving for a while instead of all the walking. They arrived back to the starting point, passing the two adults who were in the fencing truck dropping off steel posts at 30-foot intervals next to the newly stretched wire.

Ricky's truck sat off to the side. Vicente walked over to sit in the passenger seat. Scott watched. The two looked at each other for half a minute. Finally, Scott walked to the truck. "Wha'cha doin'?"

"Waiting to do some driving."

The big teen chuckled. "Come on over here. We'll be doing a different kind of driving."

The pair walked to the first steel post. Scott picked up a post driver, a pipe with a heavy weight welded to the top and handles on the side, and slid it on the post, lining it up next to the stretched wire. He lifted the heavy tool and pulled it downward with a grunt. The air rang with a deep metallic clunk from the concussion. The post entered the hard, dry ground an inch. He repeated the process for another inch, then another.

Vicente watched as the big teen drove the post into the ground with brute strength. He grudgingly admitted that the boy was big and strong. Something he himself had always wanted to be, but it was not in his genes.

The post was in the ground six inches, enough to stand upright without falling over. Scott released the heavy driver leaving it setting on the post while he stepped to the side. "I'd appreciate your helping me."

Vicente made a face. "What can I do?"

"Just stand on the other side and grab the handles. Lift when I lift and pull down when I do."

Vicente looked around as if to be away from the hard work. Seeing no other option he took hold of the driver opposite Scott. With little enthusiasm, he worked from his side. He was surprised at how much farther into the ground the post went with his help and in spite of himself, he felt pride that he was holding his own across from the football player.

When the post was 12 inches in the ground, Scott said, "Good." He then lifted the post driver off the post and carried it to the next one lying on the ground. "If you'll stand the post up next to the wire, I'll slide the driver on and we'll go again."

Vicente did as he was told, actually anxious to see how

many hits it would take to finish this post. It took six. He stood back with smug satisfaction. When Scott worked by himself, it took six hits just to go six inches.

The next post took seven hits. The one after, only five. Working together they were making good progress but were both getting tired. They had driven half of the 40 posts that needed to be driven on this quarter mile section.

Román and Ricky approached from the other direction. Each had hold of one end of a tamping bar and were unrolling a strand of wire next to the first one. Both men could see the teens working together. "How about that?" said Ricky pointing with a jerk of his head.

***

Vicente had never been so tired in all his life. He fell asleep in the fencing truck during the short ride to the ranch house. His arms ached and he scolded himself for working so hard on someone else's property. As the truck pulled into the ranch yard he observed with dismay the house still standing unscathed. Obviously his gang buddy didn't know what he was talking about. He disgustedly walked directly to the bunkhouse, took a quick shower, then fell on the bed and slept.

***

Román and Ricky leaned comfortably on the rails of the horse pen watching the horses eat. Ricky pulled a knife from his pocket and opened the blade. He slowly cleaned the dirt from under his blunt fingernails. Both men were comfortable in the silence and enjoyed the approaching dusk.

Román cleared his throat. "I appreciate your letting us come over for a few days," he thanked. "I've taken in some pretty tough boys but Vicente is the hardest yet. I was beginning to wonder if I'd bitten off more than I could chew."

Ricky studied his fingernails then folded the knife and replaced it into his pocket. "Why is it that some boys respond so well and others can't seem to understand that

94

you're just trying to help?" It was a rhetorical question so Román made no attempt to answer.

They heard the door close at the house. Both men turned to watch Jessie stroll their direction. Román stepped back. "I'm sorry, Jessie. I've imposed and now I'm cutting in on your time with Ricky."

"Not at all," she replied. "We both enjoy your company and we're so glad you came." Her expression changed. "I'm not so sure we..., at least I, feel the same about the new boy."

Román scratched the dirt with his boot toe. "I was just telling Ricky that he's a tough nut to crack." He looked up quickly. "If there's a problem I can take him and leave right now. I sure don't want to be putting you in a bind."

"No. You don't have to do that. It's just that he rubs me the wrong way. I'll keep my distance and everything will be fine."

"Are you sure? I don't want to be a bother and if he's a problem we'll head home."

Jessie shook her head. "No bother and if he's helping he's earning his keep. Sorry, I shouldn't have said anything." She glanced apologetically toward Ricky and got a shrug in return. The men accompanied her back to the house.

***

The fence building crew was hard at work on another section of fence. A fast-moving storm brought almost a half inch of rain before dawn that morning and the lingering clouds and wind kept the day cold. Vicente's sore muscles reminded him over and over how stupid he had been to have worked so hard for someone else. He wasn't going to make that mistake again.

After the first wire had been stretched to mark the straight line between the starting point and ending point, the steel posts had been laid out ready to be driven. Scott took the heavy post driver out of the fencing truck and walked to the first post.

He gazed skyward at the clouds, then along the fence

line, and finally to where Ricky and Román were shaking baling wire loose to get ready to tie the first strand to the posts. "I'll bet you a steak dinner that we can drive these posts faster than yesterday."

The men studied him from their position closer to the truck. "That's hardly a fair bet. It rained last night so the ground will be softer," countered Ricky.

"That may be true, but we're sore so it's going to be harder on us. What did it take yesterday? Just under three hours?"

"Yeah, about that. Do you think you could do it in two and a half hours?"

Vicente had been listening while leaning on the old fencing truck. Scott turned toward him. "If Vicente is willing, I'm sure of it."

All eyes turn toward the young man wearing earrings and a ball cap pulled low. This was his chance to tell them to get lost, that he wasn't going to work like a dog for them. Instead, he puffed his chest and bragged, "Two hours and fifteen minutes if *Flaco* can keep up." He gave the big teen a challenging look.

Román chuckled. "I'm in. If you two can drive all the posts by... ," he pulled a pocket watch and flipped the lid, "10:15, Ricky and I'll buy you as much of a steak dinner as you can eat." He nodded toward Ricky and got a nod in return.

"Yipee," yelled Scott. "Let's go." He held the driver as Vicente jogged to the post, held it in place, then grabbed the handles opposite the big athlete. Together the teens attacked the job, lifting as one and with all their might then pulling the driver down on the post. The loud, ringing filled the air.

When the first post was in, Vicente helped Scott lift the driver from the post, then ran ahead to get the next one in place. The bigger teen carried the tool ten steps and slid it on. A rhythm was in place and the teens were working as one. It wasn't long before the soreness of their muscles was being worked out.

Section after section, the youngsters made progress. The men started rolling out a new strand, stopping every 30 feet to tie the first wire to the newly driven posts. They watched in awe and hopefulness as their wards worked together to accomplish their goal.

"Thanks for letting us come," Román said quietly as Ricky stood from tying the wire. "This may be the turning point for Vicente. He's working hard and enjoying it for probably the first time in his life."

Ricky slipped the pliers into his back pocket and took a moment to watch the teens. "I'm glad you're here. Do you think he'll come around?"

Román remained silent, thinking of other boys that had come to him and taken advantage of their opportunities. "It's a lot like riding a colt. You celebrate the small successes but you can't expect them to change overnight. There are usually some setbacks, but two steps forward and one step back is a lot better than no steps forward."

The closer the teens got to the end, the faster they worked. Ricky and Román were close at their heels and Román called out the time every fifteen minutes. Scott called back, laughing, "I'm going to get a two-pound ribeye and still have room for banana cream pie."

"I want cherry pie and ice cream after my filet mignon," added Vicente. Both boys laughed as they ran to the next post.

"It's 9:50 and you still have four posts to go," called Román. "Don't get too cocky."

"A milk shake that we can do the four before 10:00 o'clock," bet Scott.

"You're on," agreed Ricky.

The teens were sprinting from post to post. The pleasant ringing clunk of the driver echoed from the nearby hills. The men watched in appreciation as Scott and Vicente struck the last blow on the last post, then together lifted the driver off and let it fall to the ground with a clang. As it fell, they each turned to the men. "Time," they yelled in unison, then each fell on his back to rest.

Román slowly pulled his watch from his pocket. He teasingly studied the engraving before opening the flip top. The boys rolled to a sitting position on the ground. "That's not fair," called one.

"You're cheating," cried the other.

Román studied the watch. He shook it and held it to his ear. "It must have stopped. It says 9:58."

"Yahoo!" yelled Vicente.

"Yipee," echoed Scott. The boys slapped each other on their backs then lay spread eagle on the wet ground, laughing.

Ricky turned to Román, leaned close and said, "I'd say that was two steps forward."

***

The quarter mile of fence that had been the project for the day was complete. The fencing truck was left for the next day and the two men and two boys rode back to the house in Ricky's four-door Dodge truck. Both boys were exhausted and immediately went to sleep, their heads leaning on side panels behind the doors. They were oblivious to the bouncing of the truck on the rough road.

They arrived at the ranch house just before 2:30 in the afternoon. Jessie quickly prepared them a lunch of roast beef sandwiches and cold milk. Ricky was bragging about the boys to his wife. "You should have seen it. They worked hard together and finished those posts in record time. They're getting this afternoon off as a reward."

Scott was smiling, enjoying the attention. He returned Jessie's nod and smile. Vicente, on the other hand, would not make eye contact. He knew she didn't like him and no matter how sweet she tried to be, he could feel her animosity. He ate his sandwich in silence, drawn back into the shell he had only so briefly started to break through earlier in the day.

Chapter 12

Vicente leaned on the rails of the working corrals. After the late lunch he had wanted to go to the bunkhouse to rest but since Scott had gone there he decided to stay away. He shook his head, angry with himself that he had worked so hard. Sure, they had promised him a steak dinner but how likely might that be? He didn't know what had gotten into him and he resolved to keep his distance. Román had said that after a few days on this place they would return to Roswell and his parents would come pick him up. He'd already been away past the two planned weeks though in truth he knew that the rival gang might still be looking for him so a little more time away might not be a bad thing.

The cold wind had picked up so he stepped to the board wall of the tall hay barn to be more comfortable. He sat on the sand and leaned back against the boards, absently throwing small pebbles to pass the time. Before long he closed his eyes and started drifting toward sleep when he started hearing a conversation. It was faint but whoever was talking was moving his direction so in a short time he could hear every word. It was Román and Ricky. They had walked to the wall from the opposite side and stood talking, and they were talking about him.

"I knew some time out here would do him good," It was Román. "He was a handful at my place and to be honest both Lupita and I were at our wit's end. He wasn't responding to anything we tried. Thanks for inviting us."

"My pleasure to have you here. I was beginning to wonder right at first. He didn't make a very good impression and even Jessie got her hackles up. I think it was Scott. He's the one that's the leader. Let's hope Vicente can learn from him."

The boy's face steeled into an expression of pure hatred at the sudden realization that he was a project. He had been sent by his parents not to avoid any possible danger like they had suggested, but for reformation. He was furious, first at his parents then at the men on the other side of the wall, and finally at himself. The longer he sat the madder he got.

So they wanted him to be like that big loser, Scott? He'd show them. *They ain't seen nothing yet*, he vowed to himself.

The men strolled away and the conversation was harder to make out. He was sure he heard Román say they were going back to Roswell in the morning. His relief was as instantaneous as his previous anger. *Good*, he thought. *I can't wait to be out of here and back home.*

***

Jessie stepped onto the back porch at dusk to ring the triangular dinner bell. It had been a housewarming gift from Ricky's friend and former boss, Bob, the state senator. She stood on the porch long enough to see Scott eagerly walking toward her with a huge smile on his face. She turned her attention to Vicente following slowly, at a distance. *I'll be glad when Román takes him home*, she thought. *He's a thug.*

Scott entered the kitchen taking off his hat. Ricky and Román took their customary chairs as did Jimmy Ray and Jewell. All were sitting when Vicente opened the door. He stopped, standing in the open doorway. The cold wind was blowing into the kitchen.

"Come in and shut the door," snapped Jessie.

The standing boy turned to take the door handle. In

extra-slow motion, he closed the door as he watched her expression. It was obvious she did not like him. *Good,* he thought. *That's the way I want it.*

Román, feeling the animosity, tried to break the tension. He looked at Jimmy Ray. "You know what they say. One boy is good help, two boys are no help, and three boys are like a good man gone."

Ricky laughed but the rest of the gathering sat stoically, not understanding the meaning of the phrase. "That's an old cowboy saying," volunteered the ranch owner watching the two boys and his son across the table and realizing that they had no idea what he was talking about. "What it means is that on a ranch, if one boy is there to work, he's good help because he does what he's told with no distractions. If two boys are there, the help they give is wasted as they start horsing around and not paying attention. When three boys are on the job, they are so busy paying attention to each other and getting into trouble it makes more work for everyone else. Get it? One boy's good help, two boys are no help and three boys are like a good man not showing up."

"Ah, that makes sense," replied the biggest teen. "But you won't have that trouble with us."

***

Jessie pulled the blankets back on their bed, then fluffed her pillow. Ricky sat on his side with his back to her. He had been unusually quiet all evening. She was soon to find out the reason. "Román's going home tomorrow," he mentioned.

"I'm glad. I love him but I don't like his cousin and I'm glad he'll be gone."

The young husband sat quietly tracing the pattern on the bedspread with his finger. At length, he said over his shoulder. "I told him the boy could stay." He braced for her reaction knowing full well that she would be furious and feeling guilty at the thought that he had agreed without asking her. The reaction was slow in coming. He had expected her to be angry but she made no sound. Finally, he stood and turned to face her.

Her displeasure was plain. When she spoke the sarcasm was biting. "Thanks for asking for my opinion."

He walked to her side but as he reached for her she pushed his hand away and turned to stride quickly into the bathroom. He followed her, wondering if he should try to explain or if being quiet was the best approach. She brushed her long hair, ignoring him.

He stood behind her, waiting. She stepped around him to the cabinet at his back, replacing the brush, then returned to the sink. They observed each other through the mirror.

"I'm sorry. I know you don't like him but he has made some progress. You may not be able to see it but I saw it today on the fence job." He waited for her to speak but she remained silent.

"Do you remember when I was riding the colt I called Try Again. He bucked me off more times than I'd like to admit. I was about to give up until you told me to enjoy and appreciate every small success. I did that. It took time and patience, but when he came around, he turned into one of the best colts I've ever ridden. Vicente needs a chance. He needs some celebration over any small success. Can you and I come to terms? Will you let him stay for two weeks? If he hasn't started to turn around, I'll have Román take him home."

Jessie remembered the big colt. She also remembered the many evenings she had rubbed liniment on Ricky's shoulder and back and how her exasperated husband had almost given up. She started to soften. Slowly she rubbed her fingers on the countertop. "Two weeks. But if in that time he hasn't made some noticeable gains, I get to be the one to decide if he stays or goes." She gazed at him for confirmation.

"Deal." He extended his hand for a shake but when she took it he pulled her close. He lifted her in a bear hug, her feet six inches from the floor.

Her anger dissipated slowly. He returned her to stand on the carpet then hugged her in a loving embrace. "I'm sorry. I should have asked you first."

***

In the bunkhouse, Vicente lay in his bed listening to Scott singing an off-key tune. He hadn't spoken and Scott hadn't spoken to him. *I'm glad we'll be leaving tomorrow,* he thought to himself. He reached under the bed to retrieve his suitcase so he could pack and be ready to leave. He noticed the heavy envelope his parents had sent, the one with the photo of Antonio. He hadn't opened it since that night in Roswell. He stole a quick glance at Scott. The big teen wasn't paying any attention. Vicente lifted the flap and pulled the contents. He again felt the heartbreaking loss his family had endured as he glanced at the photograph. As had been the case every time he thought of Antonio for the past four years the feeling of loss quickly gave way to anger. He glanced to make sure Scott was not watching then he slid one of the letters from the pouch. He had them all almost memorized because he had read them so many times when his brother was still alive. He remembered sitting on his bed in the little home in LA reading and re-reading the letters until the day the Marines visited. That night he put the letters away and never opened them again. He slowly unfolded the flimsy paper to read.

Hello Little Brother,

How is your freshman year in high school going? Is old Mr. Cunningham still teaching? He can be pretty funny sometimes and if you can get him talking about when he was in high school he will talk for the whole period and you won't have any homework.

I long for the cool summer nights in LA. It is hot here and I mean real hot but we are faring well. There is sand everywhere and I have to work extra hard to keep my gun clean. The Sarge said mine was the cleanest of all. He is a cool guy, not like the drill sergeant in Basic. We are all friends here and we all watch out for each other. That's the one thing I've learned so I'll pass it along to you so you'll be way ahead of me. If I had it to do over I'd be better. I'd care about others and I'd try to help when I could. So my advice to you is to be good. That's what Semper Fi means. Always Faithful. Live by the Code and everything will turn out all right.

So far all is well. We haven't had any contact to speak of with the locals though I've heard one of the units down south had a run in.

I love the Marines. Stay good,

Antonio

In bitterness he folded the letter and replaced it into the envelope. *What did the Code get you?* He questioned silently. *Nothing but killed. That's why I'm in it for me and only me. That's my code.*

***

Ricky and Jessie waved to Román in the pre-dawn darkness as he backed his truck out of the driveway and pulled onto the road toward town. They watched the tail lights grow dim in the distance then finally disappear behind the juniper trees at a bend in the road.

Turning back toward the door, Ricky grasped his bride's hand. "It'll be fine. You'll see. I'll work the boys so hard they won't have the energy to give you any trouble."

***

The boys walked from the bunkhouse for breakfast, one smiling, at peace with the world and one, wearing an Oakland Raiders cap pulled low, sullen and angry. His anger turned to concern when he noticed that his relative from Roswell was not there. He looked toward Ricky. "Where's Román?"

"He's gone back to Roswell. I asked him if it would be okay for you to stay and help us on the fence. You've been a big help and we need you to continue."

The blood drained from the young teen's face then he exploded, cursing and screaming. He left the kitchen, slammed the door and kicked a potted plant on the porch.

Jessie watched through the window as he stomped away. She was initially angry at the outburst but seeing the youngster retreat across the yard with his shoulders slumped and his head hanging, she began to feel sorry for him. The longer she watched, the more guilty she felt for disliking him so.

Out of the corner of her eye she noticed her husband watching her, waiting. She made eye contact, then with only a hint of a smile, said, "Just like old Try Again."

Ricky's relief was evident. "Yep. We'll need to celebrate every success and not dwell on the setbacks."

The couple turned in unison as they heard movement in the room. Scott had pushed his chair back from the table to stand next to them to watch Vicente through the window. All three were surprised when the furious teen walked onto the road and tiptoed across the cattle-guard toward town instead of going back to the bunkhouse.

"Where is he going?" asked Jessie.

"No telling," answered her husband, "but if he thinks he's walking to town he has a long, cold 18 miles to go. And there is no way anyone in this part of the country will give a hitchhiker dressed like that a ride."

"What shall we do?" She moved to the side window to continue watching as Vicente trudged down the road.

"Maybe we ought to let him walk a while. He can get an idea of just how isolated we are here." He paused in thought. "And it will give him a chance to think. That may be the best medicine for him right now."

The family and Scott ate breakfast then Jimmy Ray and Jewell kissed their mom on her cheek and walked to meet the bus at the county road.

The men worked around the house and barn until two hours had gone by. Scott kept watching the road, obviously concerned about Vicente. Finally, Ricky asked, "Do you think he's been out there long enough?" Though nothing was said, he could tell Scott was worried. "Okay, then, let's

jump in the truck and go get him."
***

Vicente walked on the side of the road four miles from the house. It was a cold day and the intermittent clouds blocked most of the warmth the sun offered. He heard a vehicle approaching so he turned to see who it was. The walk and the time to think had done little to calm him. He bent and retrieved a broken cottonwood limb which he swung like a baseball bat and hurled with all his strength at the big dodge four wheel drive truck coming around a bend in the road. It hit the fender just above the front wheel with a loud clang. Ricky slammed on the brakes in instant fury. The truck slid to an abrupt stop 20 yards away from the teen and the men exited quickly.

A rock hit Scott in the shoulder, then, realizing with a gasp what he had done, Vicente started running through the brush in the pasture to get away from the athlete. He ran for all he was worth but even with a 20-yard head start he couldn't outrun the big teenager. When Ricky caught up, the smaller boy was in the dirt on his back with the big boy sitting on his chest poking him with a finger. He was obviously explaining his displeasure at Vicente's actions.

The rancher was relieved that there didn't appear to be any injuries though there was an additional rip in Vicente's baggy pants and his cap was nowhere to be seen. Ricky had been concerned at the rage on Scott's face after he had been hit by the rock but it appeared that the football player had been able to control his anger.

Scott finished talking but continued to sit on the smaller boy's chest. He glanced over his shoulder to see his mentor. "You got anything to tell our friend? He's in a listening mood aren't you Vicente?"

Ricky squatted down next to the pair to address the defiant youth. "You made a good hand yesterday. You were a contributor and we enjoyed your company. I'll make you a deal. If you'll work for me for two weeks I'll call Román and you can go back to Roswell if you like. You'll get an honest day's pay for an honest day's work, a place to stay and all you can eat—and you'll have money in your pocket when you leave. How does that sound?"

"Sounds like a good deal for you. Forced labor and there's nothing I can do to get out of it." He spat the words, the anger plain.

"Maybe so, but it beats trying to walk home. Are you willing to give it a try?"

"Do I have a choice?"

"Actually, you have more of a choice than you realize. You can suck it up and make the best of it or you can be mad and miserable for the next two weeks. You're the only one that can decide."

Scott leaned down and whispered, "Go along to get along." He then stood to allow the ear stud wearing youth to do the same.

The three men quickly retreated to the truck to get out of the cold. Vicente cringed when he saw the dented fender. He expected another reproach from the ranch owner but it never came. They each got in for the silent drive back to the ranch.

As they pulled into the yard, Jessie brought out a breakfast burrito for Vicente. He took it and started eating immediately with no effort to express any appreciation.

Chapter 13

The boys were in the bunkhouse and the kids were asleep. Ricky stood, leaning on the bedroom door watching his wife get ready for bed. "You should have seen Scott when he got hit with the rock. I honestly thought he was going to tear Vicente's head off. I swear he looked like a freight train charging after the kid. I came up on them to find him sitting on Vicente and poking him in the chest, reading him the riot act. I don't know what he said but the boy worked today once we got to the fence. He may not have been happy about it but he did what he was told and kept his mouth shut. Tomorrow's Saturday and I'm going to let them work alone while Jimmy Ray and I ride."

"Do you think they'll be okay?"

He thought for a moment, imagining the possibilities, most of them unpleasant, then remembered Scott sitting on Vicente's chest. With a smile, he answered, "I think so."

***

Vicente sat on his bed. He had been non-conversational since the episode on the road toward town that morning. He had worked but only to keep that big loser from sitting on him again. He noticed Scott standing and watching him from across the room. "What do you want?" he asked sarcastically.

The big teen was quiet. He focused on his roommate. "Vicente, I'm no different than you. I'm scared for the future as much as you are. Ricky and Román are trying to help us all be better."

"I don't need no help. And don't tell me that we're the same. I didn't have no rich daddy watching out for me. Nobody ever gave me nothin'." He defiantly turned his back and sat on his bed.

Scott leaned on the door jamb. He studied his fingers for a full minute. "You think I had a rich daddy?" he asked, moving around Vicente to look him in the eye. "I don't even have a dad. He left just after I was born. I was raised by my three older sisters because my mom worked two jobs to pay the bills. My ticket out was supposed to be college on scholarship and on to the NFL, but I got stupid with drugs. It was the worst mistake of my life. I regret that but I've decided to change, to take advantage of the help Ricky is giving. Someday I want to have something, to be somebody. I've come to the conclusion that I'll never get what I really want by going down the path I was on."

Though he tried hard not to, Vicente was listening, sitting on the edge of the bed staring at the floor. He thought of the shooting in Los Angeles, the one that left his friend dead and the rival gang looking for him.

He looked to Scott, thinking about what he had just learned from his roommate, though not quite ready to change his attitude. Glancing at last toward the big boy, he said, "But you want to be here. I just want to go back home."

Scott stepped closer to tower over the rebellious young man. Quietly, he said, "Do you remember what I told you a few days ago and again this morning? You have to go along to get along. Have you ever considered that the fastest way to get home is to start acting as though you like it here? Do what you're told when you're told. No back-talk, no complaining. Who knows, in time you might come to like it here. We all have things to learn. Try for a week and see what you can pick up."

The boy on the bed rubbed his temples. "So, you think that if I pretend to like it, Ricky and Román will think I have learned my lesson and tell my parents and they'll let me go home?"

Scott cocked his head. "That's not exactly what I said but it's a start. Shall we give it a try?"

***

Mom and Dad,
Román abandoned me for slave labor on a ranch in the middle of nowhere. If you love me you will come get me.
Vicente

The letter was placed on the nightstand next to his bed. He would see if the slave driver would get it mailed. Vicente hated the ranch, hated the work and hated the people. His anger was so deep he didn't know if he could pretend to like it but after long thought he decided to take that approach in hopes it would get him home sooner rather than later.

***

Jessie concentrated on making breakfast for her family and the boys. She stood to move a pan from the stove then gazed out the kitchen window. The previous day's storm had blown through and she noticed there were some lingering clouds blocking the rising sun. Nevertheless, it appeared as though it would be a pleasant day. Her attention was drawn by movement in the yard. "Well, I'll be!" she mumbled. Through the window, she could see two teens striding toward the house.

Ricky stood next to his wife to watch, then reached over and held her close. "They look like men on a mission."

"They look like starving boys." She chuckled. "I'm going to fry some more eggs."

The door opened, the boys entered and stood behind their chairs. Jessie turned from the stove. "Y'all go ahead and start with what's on the table. I'll have some more ready in just a sec." She cracked another egg to into the cast iron skillet. It popped and sizzled in the bacon grease. Ricky turned hotcakes in another pan next to her.

The boys didn't sit, they stood patiently until the man

and wife both turned to face them. "I'm sorry," volunteered Vicente with a deferential nod. He was looking straight at Jessie. "I was out of line and it won't happen again."

She tried to read his gaze. She doubted his sincerity. After all, how could a boy change that much in only one day? She silently returned the nod, then turned to the stove and the eggs in the pan.

Ricky watched the exchange and knew right away that his wife was skeptical. He saw from the look on Vicente's face that he was thinking the same thing. *Still,* he mused, *it's a step forward.* "Thanks, Vicente. It takes a man to be willing to apologize. I'm proud of you. Now you boys eat up so you can get some work done today."

The thin teen returned Ricky's gaze. In spite of himself, he felt the tiniest surge of pride at the compliment. Then quickly coming to his senses, he thought, *I'll keep them fooled for two weeks. Then I can get out of here.*

***

After breakfast, Ricky asked Scott to come outside to the truck. Before they left he instructed Jimmy Ray to saddle a horse for the day. Once outside with the big boy, the rancher explained that he and his son would ride through the cows so he wouldn't be there on the fence crew. "You know the drill. Just keep doing what we've been doing. If we get a chance, Jimmy Ray and I'll ride over to check on you."

"Yes, sir."

"And Scott?"

"Yes."

"Make sure you keep the keys to the truck in your pocket."

They each gave the other a knowing look. "I'll do that," the big boy said with a grin.

They separated, Scott going back to the house to get Vicente and Ricky moving to the horse pen to get the buckskin colt. He was surprised as he came around the building to see Jimmy Ray sitting comfortably on Pardner.

"So, you're riding the old campaigner today I see."

"Yes, sir."

"Good for you. He probably needs ridden once in a while to stay legged up and in better shape anyway."

Ricky pulled the latigo to cinch the saddle onto the good looking colt. He led the buckskin to where Jimmy Ray and Pardner were standing, then stepped on and waved to Scott who was waiting at the truck for Vicente. He was hoping it was a good decision to send the boys to work by themselves.

The father and son rode side-by-side down the tree-lined alley, through the working corrals and out into the ocean of grass. They jogged to the west to check cows in the pasture that bordered Bob's farm. Ricky was remembering back to the days he first started riding the big black horse on that farm. He proudly glanced over to see his son capably riding that same horse. "Can I tell you a story about Pardner that I've never told anyone?"

"Sure."

"You've heard the stories of how he bucked with me every day for the first two weeks?"

"Yes, sir."

"After that he just got better and better every day. After a couple of months he and I were a team. Don't tell your mom this story, but he saved my life one day on the farm. There's a big dirt tank that the steers would sometimes get bogged down in and we would have to pull them out. The trouble was the mud was so sticky that it was hard to get out. We had gotten a rope on a big steer and started pulling him out when Pardner's leg got stuck and he fell. I was in the water under him and stuck in the mud too. I couldn't get out and I almost drowned there until I was able to grip the rope and let him pull me out. If he'd have run off I'd have drowned, but he stayed calm and got me out. He's one smart horse and I love him."

Jimmy Ray was quiet, imagining the scene. At last, he gazed at his dad with a grin as he leaned back and patted the horse on his hip.

"And talking about water," said the dad with a proud look toward his son, "I heard something on the news the other day about sharks. What can you tell me about them?"

***

Vicente left the bunkhouse and strolled toward the truck where Scott leaned with arms folded, resting in the bright winter sun. They heard the approaching truck. Both turned to watch the old Chevy with mismatched fenders roll to a stop next to the big Dodge where they waited. Vicente cocked his head, listening to the rough idle and cough as the key was turned off. He studied the truck then turned his focus to the occupants. As he saw Gabriella he blinked. She was looking at him with the biggest, darkest eyes he had ever seen. She was, he decided, probably the most attractive girl he had ever seen. He was so focused on the girl that he didn't notice Jessie watching him with a frown.

***

Three miles from the house Vicente and Scott marched forward toward the brace post that marked the ending point for the quarter mile of fence they were expected to build that day. Each was holding one end of the tamping bar. As they walked, the roll spun as the wire unreeled. At the post, they stopped to rest, dropping the bar at their feet. The late morning was cool but with no breeze and the sun shining brightly, both boys were wiping sweat from their brows.

Ten yards away sat the big Dodge truck with the dent in the front fender from the branch he had thrown. After resting for only a very short time, Vicente approached the truck and felt the dent. He studied the underside then stepped to the tool box in the back. After rummaging for only a short time, he carried a handful of tools to the front wheel. He quickly removed the heavy plastic mud guard from the underside of the wheel well and used the rounded end of a ratchet wrench to push the dent outward. It popped with a satisfying clang. He continued massaging the underside until the dent was hardly noticeable.

Scott had been tying the first strand of wire to the steel posts. He stood, stretched his back, then made his way to his companion.

The bigger teen whistled approvingly as he fingered the now almost smooth metal. "That's pretty neat. How were you able to do that?"

"Just something I picked up at home," was the answer.

The Hispanic boy kicked a pebble, uncomfortable at the attention and even more uncomfortable at the hint of the smallest feeling of pride he felt that the someone else had approved of something he had done. He quickly replaced the heavy plastic and the tools and stepped back to the roll of wire.

Scott stayed at the truck a while longer, admiring the quick repair job. He turned toward the other teen. "Are you into cars?"

Vicente shrugged his shoulders. "I guess you could say that. I like working on them."

The boys returned to their work and by 2:00 o'clock in the afternoon, were stretching the last wire when Ricky and Jimmy Ray rode up. "Looking good, men," said the ranch owner. He had ridden to the wires and was pleased with the straight, tight fence the boys had built.

"Thanks, *Patrón*," said Scott but Vicente just watched the rancher.

"We're going to ride up to Lane mill to check the water level at the storage tank there, then on to the house." The man on the buckskin colt smiled to his son then glanced back at the boys. "I'll tell you what. You only have to tie the last strand to the posts and staves. If you finish and get back before we do you can have the rest of the today and all of tomorrow off."

The boys didn't answer. They were suddenly too busy.

Ricky and Jimmy Ray laughed as they loped toward the windmill.

Chapter 14

The big Dodge was sitting in the driveway as the riders stepped off their mounts at the tack room. After unsaddling, turning their horses into the pen and carrying a bale of hay and tossing it into the feeder, the pair walked toward the house. Scott met them with a smile on his face. "Come here, *Patrón*," said the big boy pointing toward the truck.

Ricky was concerned that only Scott was there. "Where's Vicente?"

"He's in the bunkhouse, but let me show you what he did today."

The rancher was led directly to the fender. Scott rubbed the small remaining dent. "Look at this."

The cowboy was surprised as he rubbed the metal, half expecting what he was seeing to be a mirage. If he hadn't known the blemish was there it would have almost gone unnoticed. "How did he do that?"

Scott shrugged and answered, "He said he's into cars. I guess it's just something he knows how to do."

The threesome approached the bunkhouse and stepped inside. Vicente was sitting on his bed leaning against the wall reading an old Sports Illustrated magazine of Scott's. He watched as the entourage entered, wondering what it was all about.

"Thanks, Vicente," said Ricky sincerely. "I appreciate

you fixing my fender."

The young teen showed no expression. He only nodded then went back to reading—forcing himself not to acknowledge the same small feeling that was starting to grow inside. A feeling that he could contribute and that someone could appreciate him.

Just then the dinner bell rang. Everyone in the room was starving. They raced out the door, across the yard and into the house to the kitchen table.

Once they were seated, Ricky mentioned to Jessie, "These boys worked hard today. I promised them that if they finished and got back before us they could have tomorrow off. And I owe them a steak dinner from a bet earlier in the week. I was thinking we could go to San Angelo tomorrow. What do you think?"

Jessie noticed the smile on Scott's face. Vicente didn't smile but he didn't seem so defiant. She turned to her husband. "That sounds like a great idea. You boys go ahead. I was there earlier this week and would rather stay home." Then, turning to Jewell, she asked, "Will you stay home with me?"

The eight-year-old nodded with a smile. She and her mom had talked that very day after Rosalinda, Gabriella and Juanita left after cleaning the house that they wanted to take a day off and watch a good movie.

Ricky nodded then glanced at Vicente out of the corner of his eye. "While there I want to get parts to fix the jeep." He turned to the only one in the room that knew anything about cars. "Vicente, would you have time to look at it and tell me what you think it needs?"

The boy brightened until he noticed Jessie studying him so he quickly resumed his unresponsive attitude. "I guess," he said in a subdued tone.

***

The hood of the jeep was up and four bodies surrounded the engine compartment. Three were watching in the fading light while one tinkered. He checked the oil and pulled a spark plug to see the gap and check for fouling. He stood upright while wiping his hands on an oily rag. "Let's try to jump it so see what it sounds like."

The big Dodge was brought close and the cables attached. The teen in charge instructed Scott to turn the key. The jeep's starter whirred but did not turn the engine. Vicente dropped to his back and shimmied underneath. "Try it again."

He tapped the starter while the big boy turned the key. Everyone but the mechanic was surprised when the starter engaged and the engine started turning. When the motor didn't start right away, Scott released the key. "Don't stop," called Vicente. "Crank it for 30 seconds or so. I need to listen."

After the cranking, the three spectators silently observed the thin boy climb from under the jeep. He peeked once more into the carburetor then stood, once again wiping his hands on the rag. "I'll have you a list of needed parts to take to San Angelo." Though he tried to suppress it, a tiny smile appeared. He quickly looked away hoping no one saw.

***

Vicente came from the bathroom in boxer shorts and his wife-beater shirt after a shower. He strolled to the desk to sit in the chair noticing Scott sitting on his bed re-reading the same Sports Illustrated magazine he had read a dozen times before. Vicente heard the magazine plop in the bed.

"How did you learn about cars?" Scott asked.

The wooden chair made a scraping sound on the linoleum floor as Vicente turned from the desk. The football player sat on the bed in a T-shirt and sweatpants leaning against the wall with arms folded studying him.

"I learned from my dad."

"Was he a mechanic? Did he have a garage?"

"No, but he fixes cars for people after work and on weekends. He's a good shade tree mechanic and up until a few years ago I'd help him every Saturday."

"Why did you stop?"

Vicente sat quietly, thinking about the question. "Just wasn't fun anymore I guess." He looked down thinking about the last few years at home. He had always blamed the change on his brother's death but he knew down deep that the tragedy may have been the start but the gang was the real change, and it was his fault. He had wanted to fit in, to be part of a group and the gang welcomed him with open arms. Though he wouldn't admit it, he had been insecure and the escalating outbursts toward his parents or anyone in authority had been nothing more than an attempt to hide that insecurity.

He recalled his early life and the joy he had felt at being part of a loving family. The longer he hung around the gang members the less he hung around his family and the less he cared what they thought. As he remembered his early life with his family he suddenly was homesick. He wanted to sit and visit with his mom over cookies and milk like he had done in Jr. High. He wanted to lean on car fenders on Saturday mornings with his dad. He wanted to go home.

"I wish I would have had a dad to teach me things," bemoaned Scott.

Vicente didn't answer. What was there to say? He turned back to the desk, took out a paper and pen and wrote another letter.

> Mom and Dad,
> I really would like to come home. Please come get me.
> Vicente

***

Ricky sat on the living room couch digging at a sliver in his palm with his pocket knife while Jessie sat at the computer desk reading an internet article. Occasionally he heard a "Tsk, tsk, tsk," or a "hmmm," coming from her. He finally was able to get under the sliver to pull it out then he stood, replaced the knife to his pocket and stepped to her. He rubbed her shoulders and neck as he stood behind. "Whatcha reading?"

She rolled her head, enjoying the massage before answering. "An article about Los Angeles gangs. They're dreadful people."

"What does it say?" he asked while pulling a chair close to read at her side.

She scrolled up to the picture at the top of the page. A group of young men dressed exactly like Vicente glared at the camera. Their eyes were defiant and their shoulders and arms were covered in ugly, disgusting tattoos. At least two held guns and other guns and knives could be seen tucked in the waistbands of their baggy pants.

"It says the average life expectancy of a gang member is 27 years. They live violent lives and most never expect to reach adulthood. It's a life of retribution, hate and survival." She turned to look him in the eye. "Is Vicente a member of a gang?"

He thought for a time while gazing at the picture on the screen. He had to admit that the youngster dressed like the gangsters in the picture. Ricky looked through the kitchen toward the bunkhouse as he remembered the open defiance when Vicente first arrived then just as quickly recalled how much better the teen was doing. He frowned while shrugging. "I don't know. He doesn't talk much."

She studied him with a frown of her own. "Was it a mistake to have him stay?" She waited quietly for his response.

He knew she didn't like the boy and he also knew that her intuition was more often than not spot on. He, on the other hand, didn't have the gift of intuition but he had worked with Vicente. He'd seen some progress and hoped to see more. If they sent him home now the progress would be for naught and he might never get another chance.

Ricky finally answered in a soft voice. "Was it a mistake to take Scott?"

She raised her hands. "That's different. Scott's a good boy and I like and trust him."

He nodded then silently watched her. He made no effort to explain but he could see the softening of her eyes as she understood the comparison.

She dropped her head in thought. He waited patiently. Finally, she raised her eyes to his. "Okay, I'll keep quiet," she whispered while reaching for a hug.

They both jumped when the phone jangled at their side. Ricky reached to answer it. "Hello."

"Good evening," came the accented voice on the other end of the line. "This is Sylvia Zermeno from Los Angeles. I'm Vicente's mom. I got your number from Román. I hope I'm not calling too late."

"Well, hello. No, you're not calling too late. Would you like me to run out and get Vicente?" He motioned for Jessie to come closer and he held the phone so she could also hear.

"Actually, I wanted mostly to talk to you. I just want to know how he's doing. We've been getting letters that he really wants to come home but it is still too dangerous here. Is he all right?"

"You'll be happy to know that he's doing fine and working hard."

"Román said he has been a little.... defiant. Is he being too much trouble?"

Ricky looked at his wife. "Nothing we can't handle. Would you like to talk with him?"

"Yes. If it's not too much trouble."

"No trouble at all. Hold on while I run out to get him."
***

The foursome left the ranch after morning chores and a small breakfast. They didn't want to fill up too much and not be hungry for lunch though Ricky knew that would not be a problem. Scott sat in the passenger front seat while Vicente and Jimmy Ray sat, each next to a window in the back seat. The drive was pleasant and even Vicente seemed to be enjoying the trip.

Ricky wondered what the boy and his mom had talked about. He and Jessie had gone for a walk to give him some privacy and when they got back he had already returned to the bunkhouse, but this morning the boy was, if not pleasant, at least agreeable.

Ricky's wondering got the better of him so looking at the boy in the mirror he finally asked, "How was your visit with your mom last night?"

Vicente scanned the rancher's reflection in the mirror. "She said they would come get me but couldn't get away for two weeks. I'll keep working for you but when they come I'll expect a paycheck."

Ricky nodded. "We appreciate your help and you're making a good hand. I promise you'll get paid when you leave."

Vicente returned the gaze then broke eye contact to look at the scenery going by out the window leaving Ricky alone with his thoughts. He remembered the conversation with Jessie the previous evening. Despite efforts to the contrary, he found himself wondering if Vicente was only pretending. What if when they got to the city he disappeared? What if he stole a truck and took off? What if? What if? What if?

The rancher shook his head and absently rubbed the leather of the seat, deciding there were never guarantees in life. He reminded himself again to do what he could to make Vicente feel welcome and hope for the best. That was all he could do.

The first stop in town was the auto parts store where they got the parts Vicente needed for the jeep, then to the western wear store to buy Jimmy Ray some new pants. He was growing out of them faster than he could wear them out.

"Do you want some new clothes, Vicente?" asked Ricky as they pulled up. Both he and Scott turned to look back over the seat.

The teen made a face while he looked at Scott in his cowboy hat but his answer to Ricky was, if not completely respectful, was at least not disrespectful. "Nothing in a place like this that I would ever buy."

Ricky nodded but noticed that for the first time since his arrival Vicente stepped out of the truck without his Oakland Raiders cap.

Chapter 15

The attractive waitress in cowboy boots and tight pants brought their plates. True to his word, Scott ordered a two-pound ribeye. The big athlete laughed as it was placed on the table. "Now that's what I call a steak."

Vicente, also true to his word, ordered filet mignon. Ricky ordered a 16-ounce T-bone for himself and a 10-ounce one for Jimmy Ray. The meal also included all the beans and bread they could eat. Thirty minutes later, Ricky was amazed as the waitress approached and asked if they would like anything else.

"Banana cream pie for me," said Scott smugly, patting his stomach as he leaned back from the table observing his plate, empty except for the large bone.

"Cherry pie and ice cream for me," added Vicente. He not only had left his cap in the truck but he had removed the ear studs before coming into the restaurant. The rancher observed him with a half-smile.

The rancher focused on his son. "Jimmy Ray?"

The 12-year-old glanced at his plate. He was the only one that couldn't finish his meal. He shook his head. "Not for me."

Ricky nodded at the waitress. She left in a hurry and returned in just over a minute with the desserts.

As the truck pulled into the ranch driveway long after dark on that Sunday evening, the two teenagers and their pre-teen companion were asleep. All but Jimmy Ray woke as Ricky announced, "We're home boys. I enjoyed y'all's company today. Thanks for going with me." He opened his door. The interior light came on. He could see each of them squinting at the light and their recent awakening.

"Thank you, *Patrón,*" said Scott.

The driver waited for Vicente. There was no verbal thank you but the nod from the youngster was appreciated still the same.

***

The days passed quickly. It had been a week since Román had gone home leaving Vicente to work on the ranch. The boy was responding to Ricky but his relationship with the woman of the house continued to be strained. The fence work for that day was finished by 2:00 o'clock. The hungry men sat at the table while Jessie served enchiladas. The dish was one of her husband's favorites.

Vicente, having been raised on authentic Mexican food, studied his plate with an expression of disgust. He shook his head and mumbled under his breath, "That's about as sorry an excuse for enchiladas as I've ever seen." He thought he had been quiet enough but she heard and understood every word.

She roughly replaced the pan on the counter and turned with her arms folded to see him. They stared at one other, each reading in the other's eyes their mutual dislike.

"You don't have to eat it."

The boy made no attempt to lower his gaze. He continued his staring. Finally, the young mother stomped to the living room. Everyone at the table was quiet, uncomfortable at the tension. The wooden chair creaked as Ricky rose to comfort his wife. He found her sitting on the couch, her jaws clinched and her face red with anger.

"Another week is a long time. I want him gone. He doesn't like me and I don't like him. And let me remind you that I get to make the call. He can stay this last week but after that he's not welcome here."

The rancher sat on the couch with an arm around her shoulder and pulled her close. "All right. I'll have Román come to get him next week."

Two days later, Scott sat on a bucket watching Vicente work on the jeep, occasionally handing him a wrench or anything else he asked for. No one had asked the young man to do the repairs, but since it was something he enjoyed he did it anyway, if for no other reason than to make the time go by more quickly.

Ricky strolled to the jeep from the barn where he had been oiling one of his saddles. He saw the man on a bucket and noticed two skinny legs in baggy pants sticking out under the bumper. He said nothing but winked at Scott. The big teen nodded as Ricky turned and ambled to the house.

***

Another day of routine, boring fence work. It was Saturday and Jimmy Ray was helping. The good news was that the fence was almost completed. The rancher had taken his truck back to the house for additional steel posts. When he returned, the three boys were nowhere to be seen. He called but received no answer so he honked the horn.

He started getting concerned until he saw them approaching over the top of a hill a quarter mile away. They were obviously enjoying each other's company, laughing and joking and pushing each other playfully as they ambled down the hill.

"Where have you been?" asked the ranchman as they approached.

Scott spoke, "I saw some caves over there so we went to check them out."

Ricky looked at the three young men then at the fence section for the day in the earliest stages of completion. "Three boys are like a good man gone," he quipped softly with a smile, remembering the old cowboy saying that Román had shared.

***

The days passed quickly. The boys were getting faster at fence building so they were able to build more each morning. The afternoons were spent watching Vicente work on the jeep. Ricky, Jessie, and Jewell sat on the porch on Friday afternoon. Dinner was in the oven so they took advantage of a beautiful winter day. They could see from their vantage point, the teenagers and Jimmy Ray surrounding the engine compartment of the jeep.

"Do you think he'll be able to get it to run?" she asked.

"Nah. That old jeep hasn't run for at least four years. The only reason I bought the parts he wanted was to see if it would keep him busy. It's served its purpose. He's actually been pleasant for the most part and good help on the fence crew."

Jessie gazed at her husband. Her interactions with the boy had continued to be strained. He never said please or thank you and acted like he expected her to wait on him hand and foot. She reluctantly admitted to herself that she hadn't given him much of a chance. He just rubbed her the wrong way and she just didn't like him. The two weeks would be up in two days and she was looking forward to having him gone.

Scott strolled to where they were sitting. "*Patrón*, can I borrow the keys to your truck to jump the jeep?"

The rancher looked up in surprise. "Does he think it'll start?"

"He thinks so."

The family of four watched from the porch as the teens attached the cables. They could hear the cranking of the engine. When it didn't start they watched Vicente climb onto the fender and tinker with something. As he stepped down, the cranking started again. The smug expression on Ricky's face turned immediately to surprise as the engine roared to life.

"Yipee," yelled Scott as he slapped the mechanic on the back.

***

The interior of the bunkhouse was dark and a gentle snoring, mingled with the ticking of the old clock on the wall could be heard. Scott was asleep but Vicente was awake. He lay on his back in the bed staring into the darkness toward the ceiling. The elation he had experienced at the starting of the old jeep had lingered and he smiled at the thought. He contemplated the slap on the back from Scott. It had been nothing more than an instant reaction from the big boy but to Vicente it had meant a great deal as they had shared in the joy of the moment. He reluctantly admitted that he liked the football player. He didn't know why, they had nothing in common and they had definitely started off on the wrong foot. He wondered if it was because the big boy had accepted him for who he was and made no judgements. They had had their difficulties but Vicente confessed to himself that they had been of his own making. He also enjoyed working with Scott. He was treated as a contributor and his help seemed to be appreciated.

He thought again of the letter from Antonio with the admonition to be good and he suddenly wondered just where he fit in that respect. He realized he had never been a bad boy but here in the middle of nowhere, he'd come to the conclusion that since hanging with the gang he hadn't been a good boy either. The introspection was uncomfortable. He would be going home soon and all this would be a distant memory. He wanted to think it would be a bad memory but caught himself in time. It hadn't been so bad, he decided. To a degree, it had started out as slave labor but Ricky had been true to his word, all he could eat and money in his pocket. He realized with some pride that without him the fence would be far from finished and he had enjoyed listening to the rancher's stories.

He carefully slipped out of the bed and pulled his pants on. He smiled as he tied the knot of the soft cotton rope he used as a belt. He put on his tennis shoes over bare feet and silently crept out the door. To his left was the security light casting a bluish glow in a circle at the base of the pole in the dark, moonless night. Close to the light was the horse corral. He strolled to it and leaned on the fence. The big black horse came to the fence to smell his hands.

"Nothing for you to eat," said Vicente, smiling while he rubbed the horse's forehead. He'd heard Ricky's stories about the horse and the trouble they'd had when they first started and how the horse came to trust Ricky and never looked back. He wondered if perhaps he was a little like the horse in that respect. He had come unwillingly and wanted no part of ranch life, only the security of knowing he was far from the danger that faced him in LA.

He recognized that though he hadn't particularly enjoyed the work he had enjoyed the comradery and the occasional compliment. He also recognized the feeling he had long forgotten, the feeling of satisfaction that comes from seeing the progress from a job well done.

He had felt that before but it had been a long time, not since Jr. High when he still helped his dad with the cars or his mom with the garden. He thought of his parents and remembered their worried looks in his behalf. He had ignored them, too tough to acknowledge that he was causing them pain.

He rubbed the black horse one more time then strolled away from the light toward the old yellow jeep that sat just outside one of the barns. Away from the security light he was able to see the stars twinkling overhead. He was amazed at the clarity and brilliance of the countless stars in the sky. He hadn't seen that in LA.

At the jeep he rubbed his fingers over the fender then stepped onto the running board then into the seat. He sat in quiet contemplation for the better part of an hour before sneaking back into the bunkhouse and over to his bed. Scott was still snoring. Vicente lay on the bed, interlaced his fingers behind his head and smiled.

Chapter 16

The next day the last gate in the last section of fence was in place. Ricky bragged to the builders. They all piled into his big Dodge but the road he took was not the road back to the ranch. Instead, he drove to a hill three quarters of a mile away. "Come on," he said as he exited.

The boys looked at each other for a hint but neither knew any more than the other. They followed the rancher. After climbing the hill for 100 yards, he stopped to allow his followers to catch up. They stood in a group.

"You boys have done an outstanding job working for me this past couple of weeks." Then pointing toward the new fence, each could see it lined up with their position, stretching toward the horizon straight, true and tight.

Each felt a surge of pride, but none more than Vicente. He had driven the posts and stretched the wire and there it stood, a job completed, not a post out of line, every wire tied evenly and tight. He couldn't explain the emotion he was feeling at this very moment. He had worked alongside them as an equal. He didn't have to prove anything, they accepted him and had appreciated his contribution.

No one in the group spoke for a full minute, they simply stared at the fence and reveled in the feeling of a job well done. Vicente surprised them as he spoke and the surprise was amplified at his words. "Thank you... *Patrón.*"

The effect on Ricky was electric. He reached to shake

the young man's hand then pulled him close for an embrace. When he released the youth, he saw tears welling in the boy's eyes. He looked away quickly to keep from embarrassing him, then hugged Scott.

"Y'all are good boys. Don't ever let anyone tell you otherwise."

***

The couple sat in the living room, each on one of the matching rocker/recliners. The boys had gone to the bunkhouse and the kids had gone off to bed. They were finally alone. Ricky had been anxious all evening to tell Jessie about the afternoon but before he could start, she said, "The two weeks is up tomorrow. Are you going to call Román to tell him to come get the boy?"

His head dropped. He had been hoping that his wife and the boy could come to terms. He had seen a remarkable change in Vicente but obviously she hadn't come to the same conclusion. "He called me *Patrón* today for the first time. You may not see it but he has come a long way."

"I'll admit that he's not so belligerent but I still don't like him. You remember our deal. I get to make the decision. You're finished with the fence so you don't need the help. I think it's for the best if he goes home."

"Very well." His shoulders sagged. He knew it would do no good to argue and he had agreed that it was up to her to say if the boy could stay. She had agreed to the two-week trial and for that he was grateful. He had seen a change in Vicente and hoped the boy had been able to recognize it also.

He reached for the phone then dialed the number. Jessie went to the kitchen. She wasn't in the mood to hear him tell Román what a great boy Vicente was.

He watched her go as the phone rang and was answered in Roswell. "Hello, Román. How are you tonight?"

"I'm good my friend. How are things with you?"

"Couldn't be better. We finished the fence. The boys worked hard and did a good job but the two weeks we agreed to keep Vicente is up. I'm just calling to have you make arrangements to pick him up."

"I can do that. I appreciate you keeping him. How did he do? Since I didn't hear from you I hopefully assumed he was doing fine."

Ricky paused before answering. "He was a challenge for the first little bit. Scott did a great job of keeping him in line. I could see small changes but today was the biggest change. He called me *Patrón*."

"That is a change. Sounds like you worked some pretty good magic."

"I don't know about that. I think it was more the isolation and hanging around with Scott. I hope you'll be able to see the change and I hope he keeps it up."

"Me too. Would it be too much trouble to ask him to come to the phone?"

"Not at all. Hang tight and I'll jog out to call him in."

He quickly exited through the kitchen door, reaching to touch his wife on the shoulder as he passed. He knocked on the bunkhouse door then opened it. "Vicente, Román's on the phone. He wants to talk to you."

The boy shuffled past the rancher. He was embarrassed at what had happened earlier that afternoon. He wouldn't meet Ricky's gaze. He entered the house through the kitchen, stopping briefly as he saw Jessie sitting at the table reading a magazine. Their eyes met. Each looked at the other. There was no hello, no nod of greeting and no smile. They simply stared at each other until the husband, who had been only a few steps behind, walked through the door. The teenager wordlessly passed through the kitchen to the phone.

Ricky sat next to his wife at the table, reaching to hold her hand. "He said he would come get him."

She watched the man she had grown to love so much. She could plainly read in his eyes that he hated to send the boy away. He had mentioned that Vicente was making progress. Unfortunately, she did not see it. *If only the boy wasn't so stubborn,* she thought to herself. Then in a flash of insight, she wondered if maybe she was also being stubborn. *Oh well, it doesn't matter now. He'll be gone tomorrow and that will be that.*

Vicente entered the kitchen. "He said he wants to talk to you again."

The rancher gave his wife's hand a squeeze as he got up. He winked, then followed by the young man, strolled to the living room. "Hello."

"Have you talked with him about me picking him up?"

The cowboy gazed at the boy as he spoke into the phone. "No, we all agreed on two weeks, they will be up tomorrow."

"It's hard for me to believe, but he said if it's all the same, he'd like to stay there a little longer."

Ricky's gazed toward the youngster. He held his hand over the mouthpiece. "You want to stay?"

Vicente rubbed his left thumb, then looked up at his boss. He nodded his affirmation.

"I'll call you back." Ricky replaced the phone then addressed the thin boy sitting on the couch. "Are you sure?"

Vicente had been struggling with this decision for the past two days. He had known the two weeks was coming to an end and that knowledge had brought up a myriad of conflicting emotions. He wanted to go home but as he thought about his mom and dad, he was ashamed at the way he had treated them. He realized that the friends he hung around with were not good influences and he also realized that for at least the past week, he had been doing a lot of thinking about the future, his future.

Something Scott had said echoed over and over in his mind. "Vicente, I'm no different than you. We're scared for the future as much as you are. Ricky and Román are trying to help us all be better."

He looked his boss directly in the eye. "If you'll let me, I'd like to stay."

The man of the house stood as a slow smile crept

across his face. "I'd be glad to have you stay but you'll have to get permission from the highest authority." He pointed toward the kitchen.

The teen swallowed hard, then with head down, said, "She hates me."

"All you can do is try to set things right. I'm sorry, but she has the final say."

The teen left his new boss and shuffled into the kitchen without a hint of the bluff and bluster he had exhibited when first brought by Román two and a half weeks earlier. She eyed him as he approached and leaned, two-handed, on the chair directly across from her seat. She noticed that his hair was combed and he no longer wore the ear studs. Their eyes met.

"I've come to apologize for the way I've been acting. I've been a jerk and I'm sorry."

She made no reply, she simply sat and studied him across the table. She was trying to determine if he was sincere. He had apologized once before but it had been just a ploy. He hadn't really meant it. Somehow, this time felt different. She could sense the humility, something she had not felt from him. And his eyes were different also. The defiance was no longer there. He seemed truly sorry for the way he had acted but in spite of that she was not ready to accept that he had really changed or if this may be another ploy.

"Apology accepted," she said with no enthusiasm. She went back to reading, expecting him to leave. When he didn't, she glanced up again to see him studying her. "Is there something else?"

The young man took a deep breath while nervously rubbing the top of the chair with both thumbs. "Would it be okay with you if I stayed a while longer?"

She frowned. "I thought you wanted to go home. Don't you hate it here?"

He returned her gaze, unwilling to immediately answer. She studied him. The tough guy attitude with which he had arrived seemed to be gone now. She suddenly recognized, standing in front of her, a scared boy. Scared of being a loner, scared of being left behind and scared of a future that seemed no brighter than his past. She didn't know how she knew these things, but she was mostly certain she had read him correctly. Still, there was enough of a doubt that she reserved judgement.

He shifted his weight from foot to foot then slowly licked his lips. "I did, but I have friends here now and something to do. Something that makes me feel useful, appreciated. I've never had that before."

"Do you really want to stay?" she asked with a tone signaling that she didn't trust him or believe what he was saying.

"Yes, ma'am. I do."

It was Jessie's turn to look away. It must have been beyond difficult for him to come and talk to her knowing how much she disliked him and she had to admit that the last couple of days he had been easier to get along with— but she doubted his sincerity. How could a thug change so quickly? It had to be an act. He can't be sincere.

"Ricky," she said looking toward the living room. "You can come out from behind the wall now."

She had guessed correctly. He had been hiding behind the wall at the opening from the kitchen to the living room. He stepped out immediately. "Well?"

She returned her focus to the young man. Her face held no hint of acceptance, no expression of sympathy and no smile. "Will you excuse us for a while?" she requested in a flat tone.

Vicente nodded, slumped his shoulders then looked at the floor. With a final glance of hopeless desperation at the lady of the house, he turned and plodded through the kitchen and out the door.

The couple in the room watched him go. After the door closed she turned to her husband. His eyes were pleading but he held his tongue. She waited for the expected 'please let him stay' but he continued his silence. The longer he stood without speaking the guiltier she felt for her dislike of the boy. She took a deep breath and got suddenly angry at Ricky's silence. *Dang him, he always did that but I'm not going to give in this time.* "Ricky, he's a thug and I don't want him around. He's just biding his time till he can steal a truck and he'll be long gone." She flipped the magazine she had been reading to the table. It landed with a plop and both looked at it absently. Suddenly she remembered his unabashed staring at Gabriella. She looked up at her husband. "And there's another reason he needs to go."

Ricky pulled a chair from under the table and sat facing her. He reached for her hand and held it lovingly but continued his silence. She saw his questioning expression.

"Gabriella," is all she said.

His expression became more puzzled.

"You weren't here the other morning but he was. When he saw Gabriella he stared at her like a hungry wolf. She's a nice girl and certainly doesn't need the likes of him sniffing around."

She sat rigid as she heard the cluck of his tongue and watched him shake his head, but her resolve weakened when she saw his dropped head and sagging shoulders. He pushed tiredly out of the chair.

"Okay. I'll call Román back right now." He turned to wander into the living room.

She held her head in her hands as she slumped at the table. She hated to treat Ricky like this and she wondered why she disliked the boy so. She realized that her comment about Gabriella was groundless. They hadn't even spoken on that day. She admitted that it was possible that she hadn't really given the boy a chance though she was instantly angry that she was the one feeling guilty.

She heard the beep of the phone as Ricky punched the buttons. "Okay," she heard herself say. "He can stay."

There was no sound from the other room for a full 30

seconds. She stood to peek around the corner to see Ricky sitting with head down absently rubbing the phone with his thumb. She stepped to the side of the recliner then sat on the armrest. He looked up and studied her face.

"You don't have to give in. It's your decision and I'll honor it."

She lightly rubbed his face. "Is he really doing that much better?"

He nodded then put his hand on her knee and gave a loving squeeze.

She hugged his neck then with a thought quickly stood and faced him. She pointed her finger at his nose and said, only half in jest, "Keep him busy outside working and away from me. He can stay but don't expect me to be his friend."

Ricky stood and grinned at her and she could tell he knew the request was sincere.

"I can do that. Anything else?"

She paused for only half a second. "If he stays he has to get real clothes. No more baggy pants. Every time I see him I want to pull my own pants up."

Her husband's grin broadened and he chuckled and nodded. "I'll make sure he agrees to that. I feel the same way."

She studied him, noticing his black hair falling over his brow and his dancing eyes. She wanted to squeeze him every time he grinned and cocked his head like that. She realized for the thousandth time how much she loved him. She stepped closer and wrapped her arms around his neck again and pressed her face into his chest. "I'm sorry I'm being stubborn."

He held her tenderly, returning her embrace and rubbing her long hair. "I love you so much."

"I love you too," she replied, looking up into his face.
***

Ricky strolled through the kitchen, out the door and along the path to the bunkhouse. He knocked on the screen door and entered at the beckoning from inside. He glanced at Scott sitting at the head of his bed, ankles crossed and hands clasped behind his head. Both nodded then each in turn focused on Vicente.

The teen had ignored the ranchman's entrance. He stood facing the opposite direction with head down. In front of him was his suitcase into which he had placed all his belongings.

"Vicente," Ricky called softly.

The boy turned to look at the man he had grown to respect. "Yes, *Patrón*. I already know the answer. I'm packed and ready for Román to come get me. I'm sorry to have caused you trouble."

Ricky shook his head then brightened. "She said you can stay."

Vicente cocked his head in disbelief. "She said I could stay?"

"Yep." He watched the boy and the confusion on his face.

"But she hates me?"

Ricky started to disagree but realized that what the boy had said was too close to the truth for denial though maybe extreme dislike would have been a better term. He studied the youngster for the briefest instant and thought he could detect the faintest glint of hope in those dark eyes. "She doesn't hate you but if you stay you should probably stay out of her way."

The bed creaked as Scott sat up. The men each glanced at him. He smiled and nodded encouragement toward Vicente.

The youth stared hopefully at the big teen on the bed then focused on the ranchman with the same gaze. "I can do that. I'll even eat here in the bunkhouse."

Ricky chuckled. "You must really want to stay."

Vicente got serious. "I do."

Ricky breathed deeply. "You can still eat at the house but there is one other thing," he paused. "You can't wear those clothes anymore."

Vicente looked quickly down at the wife-beater t-shirt and the baggy pants held up by the soft cotton rope he'd been given the first day. He returned his gaze to the man. Slowly, the corners of his mouth raised and his smile expanded naturally. *"No problema, Patrón,"* he agreed sincerely.

The rancher gave the boy a thumbs-up signal along with a sincere smile. "Now, come back to the house and call your folks and make sure it's okay with them if you stay."

Part Two

A Time to Take

Chapter 17

Ricky looked away and closed his eyes as he held the steel in his gloved hands, pressing it in place and holding it while Vicente jerked his head down causing the welding hood to fall over his face. A second later the portable welding machine growled as it increased power in response to Vicente's welding. The corrals next to the ranch house were made of pipe and steel and looked to be invincible but with years of cows leaning on rails or horses kicking gates, occasional upkeep was necessary.

"Got it," said Vicente as the first of the weld solidified, holding the rod in place.

Ricky stepped back, standing behind Vicente out of the glare of the bright, blue light while the boy completed the task. He smiled at the boy's back, noticing Wrangler jeans, round toed, low-heeled boots and a snap up western shirt under the leather welding jacket. Ricky had been happy that the boy had not complained about trading in his gangster clothes for the cowboy garb on the first possible day for all to go to town.

"Try these on," instructed the San Angelo western wear store employee handing a pair of pants to the young man. She had frowned in disgust at the sight of Vicente strolling through the door. The frown was not lost on the young man though he had no reaction. She brightened considerably when Ricky, Scott and Jimmy Ray followed.

In the changing booth, Vicente sat on the bench

holding the Wrangler jeans. He fingered the stiff material while thinking about the baggy pants he was about to remove. He remembered the times back in LA that he had to hold his pants up with one hand and how annoying that had been. He wondered how the low-pants fad had ever gotten started in the first place. He realized he had started wearing them just to fit in, to feel wanted and to be a part of something, a family of sorts, then he wondered if he was changing his style now for the same reason.

Yes, he realized, but then just as quickly he came to the conclusion that at least this was a family he suddenly craved to be a part of—a constructive, loving, hard-working family. A family like he had been a part of in his early years.

In a moment of sudden regret, he was homesick for his mom and dad. They were good people and he had let them down. He could see it now and was ashamed at the way he had acted. They had sacrificed so much for him and he had taken it for granted. It was all about what he wanted, no matter the cost to them. He remembered the funeral and the following weeks of quiet torture in the house. There was nothing to say. He savagely removed the wife-beater and threw it on the floor. *A month or more here then I'll go back and make them proud,* he decided.

That afternoon he noticed Jessie walking to meet the men as the truck pulled into the driveway. Ricky stepped out and kissed her then both turned to watch Vicente come around the front of the truck in his new clothes. He looked at her with a blank face though what he hoped for was some sign of acknowledgement, of approval. He saw Ricky's grin from the corner of his eye, but her face was impassive, unreadable. There was no hint of acceptance and she quickly looked to the other boys. Her smile toward them only added insult to injury for Vicente. He dropped his head and made his way to the bunkhouse.

Mom and Dad,

Thanks for letting me stay a while longer here in Texas. I'm helping out on the ranch though mostly

what I do is mechanic work and some welding. Thanks Dad for teaching me. I'll come home in the Spring.
Vicente

He reread the quick letter before folding it and placing it in the envelope. *Why is it so hard to say what I want to say?* He shook his head then licked the flap and sealed the letter.

***

Ricky listened to the welding machine throttle down as Vicente completed the weld then lifted his hood and stepped back to view his work. The sun was almost to touch the horizon in the west and the sky was painted crimson, orange and purple. Ricky touched the young man's shoulder. "Good work. Now, let's get rolled up and go in for supper. The two men rolled the cables onto the welding trailer and picked up any trash or spent welding rod. They were met by Scott and Jimmy Ray, who had just finished feeding all the animals.

Scott strolled to the weld and whistled. "I wish I could do that?" he mentioned wistfully."

Vicente stood straighter in obvious pride. "I could teach you."

"Really?"

"Sure."

Jimmy Ray stepped closer. "Me too?"

Vicente glanced at Ricky and received a nod in return. "You bet."

***

Gabriella and Juanita skipped down the steps from the bus for the daily half mile walk from the county road to their modest home. The short southwestern winter was coming to an end and the day was pleasantly warm. The weeds grew easily at the side of the two-track road as well as in the middle where no tires ever passed. The girls walked side-by-side, each on a bare and dusty 16-inch wide bald track. Though their ages were eight years apart and they had polar opposite personalities, they were best of friends and Juanita looked up to her sister as one of the wisest women in all the world. Juanita chattered incessantly during the ten-minute walks to and from the bus each day while Gabriella smiled and listened, only occasionally offering any comment.

Juanita rambled on about a boy in her class who had sat with her during lunch. Gabriella half-listened with feigned enthusiasm while thinking of her own school experiences for the past 12 years. She loved this valley and the people here. She was treated as an equal even though she was the daughter of possibly the poorest man in the valley. She shook her head at the thought, then noticed that Juanita had stopped talking and was looking at her with a questioning expression.

"I'm sorry, what did you say?" she asked as they strolled leisurely down the road. The two sisters always spoke English to each other but always Spanish when their parents were in the conversation and often when talking to their brothers.

Juanita shifted her backpack while staring at her sister. "I asked if you have a boyfriend?"

Gabriella chuckled then looked away in the distance. "No. I don't have a boyfriend. Why do you ask?"

"Cause Billy says his brother thinks you're pretty."

Gabriella pursed her lips in thought. "Billy who?"

"Billy Tompkins, the boy that sat next to me at lunch."

The older sister grinned as she realized that Billy Tompkins' brother was only a freshman but she was flattered nonetheless.

Their thoughts were interrupted and both girls turned in unison as they heard a vehicle approaching from the rear. It was an older Ford and both recognized it right away as Alonzo's truck. Alanzo was the brother immediately older than Gabriella. He worked for a big ranch only a hundred miles or so away. They stepped into the short weeds at the side of the road to let him pull even. As the truck stopped he motioned for them to jump in for a ride to the house.

Juanita got in first then Gabriella. "*Hola,* Alonzo," they both said.

Alonzo, usually cheerful and happy was sullen and his only response was a nod.

"What's wrong," questioned Gabriella upon seeing his attitude. The conversation continued in Spanish.

Alonzo glanced at Juanita then back to the older sister. "Nothing. I just need to talk to Mom and Dad."

Their little flock of chickens scattered with excited cackles as the Ford truck rolled to a stop in the dirt driveway. Their mother, who had been hanging clothes on the line came quickly over to welcome her son. Her rotund face was the picture of happiness until she saw Alonzo. "What is the problem?" she asked.

As in the truck, he glanced quickly at the youngest daughter then shook his head. "It is nothing Mama. When will Papa be home?"

Rosalinda habitually looked toward the sun. His job on the ranch up the road had been his first full-time job since coming to Texas and he almost always got home just before dark. "Not long," she answered.

"I will tell you when he comes."

He took her arm and led her back to the clothesline to help her hang clothes while the girls hurried into the house to change clothes so they could do their chores. The schedule was always the same. Home from school, chores till dark, dinner then homework and finally showers and to bed. They had no TV, no computer and no phone.

Juan arrived in the old truck with different colored fenders immediately after the sun set over the hills to the west. He greeted Alonzo with a hug and frowned at his son's attitude. Finally, after the dishes were washed he listened to Alonzo's whispering in his ear. Juan turned to Juanita. "*Mi Hija,* we have some grown-up matters to discuss. Would you please do your homework in your room?"

The eight-year-old shrugged then gathered her backpack from the floor and retreated to the bedroom she shared with Gabriella. The small home only had two bedrooms. When the boys still lived at home they always slept outside under a lean-to.

Gabriella studied the faces of her parents and Alonzo as they sat around the scarred, wooden table. Alonzo breathed deeply as he looked at his folks and sister. "Eduardo was picked up by the Border Patrol."

The parents looked quickly toward each other. Their greatest fear in all the years had been the Border Patrol and all the children knew it. They had never had any problem in this valley because it was so remote and the ranchers and farmers here would never call to report an illegal. Eduardo worked on a vegetable farm and greenhouse facility close to Abilene and to their knowledge this was the first time he, or any of them, had been detained.

"What happened?"

"I don't know the whole story but I understand the facility was raided and almost 50 were loaded into vans and taken away."

"Why the sudden raid? Did someone report them?" The complete dejection in Juan's voice was evident for all to hear.

"I hear it is the *Federales*, a new boss over this region and he wants to make a show."

"Where is Eduardo now?" asked the anxious mother.

"Near as I can tell he is in what they call processing and will be deported within the week, but don't worry about Eduardo, he'll be back in a matter of days."

Gabriella saw the relief in her parent's faces and she was sure her expression was the same. She had so many questions but it was not her place to talk or ask anything so she sat quietly waiting for more information.

"Then why the sad face?" asked Juan.

Alonzo rubbed a place on the table where a black burn on the wood showed where long ago a hot pan had been placed without any pad or protection. He looked deep into his dad's eyes. "It is because this valley is in the new man's region. I am worried he will send agents here and that you might be in danger."

Gabriella shuddered at the thought. Suddenly the desire to somehow go to college had been completely washed away and replaced with the fear, the fear of arrest and deportation to Mexico. She had been born in Mexico but had only lived there for the earliest part of her life. In fact, she couldn't remember ever being there. What would they do if arrested? Would they be able to make their way back as easily as Eduardo?

Her eyes snapped wider. What if they were separated? What if they couldn't make it back? What if instead of deportation they were sent to prison? She shook her head, terrified at the possibilities.

***

As terrified as Gabriella was, Juanita was even more so. She had retreated to the bedroom as she had been told but her curiosity was overpowering. She crept to the hall to lean on the door jamb leading to the kitchen. She heard every word. A tear rolled down her cheek as she imagined with horror a group of soldiers rounding them up like cattle and hauling them to Mexico. Her imagination was working overtime and she couldn't control it. In her mind's eye she saw herself in a strange town in Mexico and her mom, dad, and sister taken away. They called for her to join them but she couldn't move. It was as though she was stuck in deep mud. They were gone and she was alone, eight-years-old and frightened beyond belief.

She turned and stumbled down the short hall and without thinking walked out the back door and into the ranchland beyond. She walked without conscious thought of where she was or where she was going. The terrifying movie in her mind of her aloneness was all she could see. She walked for minutes or hours, she couldn't tell. The night was dark and cold though she took no notice.

Her fragile mind had been pushed to the breaking point and the imagined experiences gripped her so tightly that she was beyond reason. Unconsciously she walked into the night, skirting juniper trees and brush. A half mile from their little house the girl stepped around a small oak tree and was immediately swallowed by the earth. An anomaly of nature, a crevasse had opened sometime in recent history—a sheer-sided crack in the earth six feet wide, ten feet deep and 30 feet long. She fell headlong into the abyss hitting her head soundly on an ancient tree limb at the bottom. Her limp body settled on the soft sand at the bottom.

Chapter 18

Gabriella listened intently as her brother explained the real reason for his visit. "You need to make some plans in case you are detained. You can make your way back but the worry is if you get separated. You should know where you might meet, who you might call and what you might do. What if they came while the girls were in school? Is there someone you could call?" He looked straight at Gabriella. "Is there somewhere you could take Juanita while you wait for news of mom and dad?" You should memorize phone numbers and be prepared just in case."

"What about Juanita, she was born in this country?" asked Rosalinda remembering with no pleasure the harried ride to Carla's house eight years earlier.

"Did you get a birth certificate?"

She frowned. "No."

"Then she is in the same boat as the rest of us."

The next 45 minutes was spent discussing plans for different scenarios and though still frightened, the little family felt somewhat better about having a plan.

"I'll sleep in the lean-to," announced Alonzo as his chair squeaked as he pushed it back from the table. "Good night." He hugged his parents and Gabriella before leaving the room.

Juan and Rosalinda heavily trudged toward their

bedroom, the weight of their family's illegal status heavy on their minds. Gabriella strolled to her shared room expecting to see Juanita asleep in the middle of the shared bed. It happened every time the young sister went to sleep before her. To her surprise, Juanita wasn't in bed. She scanned the tiny room then stepped to the hall and bathroom. No Juanita.

Concerned, she walked through the kitchen to her parent's bedroom door and knocked softly.

"Yes?" Juan questioned.

"Juanita is not in the house," she said. She heard the bed springs creak then his soft footfalls on the wooden floor, then the door opened. He stood in front of her barefooted in a t-shirt and pants.

"Not in the house?" he questioned.

"No, sir."

Rosalinda joined them in the hall. Together they walked through the kitchen to look through the door to the girls' bedroom. "Juanita," they called, softly at first but louder and more frantically as the seconds passed. Juan pushed through the back door to the makeshift porch where the old washing machine rested in the corner. He yelled loudly, "Juanita? Juanita, were are you?" There was no answer.

Alanzo appeared from the lean-to. "What is it?"

"Juanita is not in the house. Have you seen her?" asked Juan louder than was needed.

The son shook his head. "Not since supper."

For the next hour they searched in vain, more worried as each search took them farther from the house. They yelled into the darkness until their voices were strained and hoarse. Their small flashlight, dim at best in the beginning, had died. For a time they used candles and their single kerosene lamp kept in a cupboard for when the electricity went out. Finally in desperation Juan whispered to Rosalinda that he was going for help.

The small family gathered at the truck and all crossed

themselves after a quick prayer for guidance uttered by the wife, the most devout of them all.

Juan stepped into the truck and turned the key. The starter groaned then engaged, cranking the tired old engine. He pumped the gas pedal and slapped the steering wheel. No luck. He tried again after allowing the starter to rest for a few seconds. As before the cranking was loud in the stillness of the night but the engine would not start.

"Take my truck," insisted Alonzo, opening the door and literally pulling his father from the truck and pushing him toward his Ford. To their relief, it started and Juan left in a spray of gravel and dirt on his way to the nearest neighbors two miles away.

***

Jessie quietly rolled from the bed and felt her way along the wall toward the door in the dark bedroom. Ricky's snoring was worse tonight than usual and she couldn't sleep. Her husband had the luxury of being able to go to sleep at the drop of a hat, and he did almost every night. Jessie had long since given up trying to have conversations with him while lying in bed. Tonight, as was the case in too many nights over the course of their marriage, he was asleep in minutes while she replayed the events of the day over and over in her mind.

Tonight she had been thinking of Vicente. It had been four weeks since she had agreed to allow him to stay. They had silently reached an agreement of sorts. As much as possible he stayed away from her and she stayed away from him. They were far from friendly though she admitted he wasn't quite so repulsive since he had gotten rid of those gangster clothes.

The boys had been repairing corrals and building a new set of smaller working corrals at one of the windmills so she only saw them in the mornings for breakfast and the evenings for supper. She felt better as long as he was with Ricky and Scott and away from the house, but they had finished the new corrals that very day, making her wonder if he was going to be skulking around the house until Ricky could find another job away from the headquarters.

She found the door and slid out as quietly as possible, closing it behind her as she reached for the light over the stairs. She blinked at the sudden brightness then made her way down the stairs and into the living room. She pushed the power button for the computer then jumped in fright as the phone suddenly shrilled at the computer's side. She placed her hand over her racing heart and tried to calm her breathing. "Hello," she answered.

"Hi, Jessie. This is Bob."

Before she could respond she heard a click then Ricky's groggy voice on the upstairs phone.

"Hello."

"Hi, Ricky," greeted Bob. "I'm glad you're both on the line. Juan and Rosalinda need some help. Their little girl is missing and we're getting up a search party. Can you load some horses and go to their place?"

Jessie quickly thought of the happy eight-year-old and of the times she had come to play with Jewell. Her heart sank at the thought of the young girl, lost and afraid. Unconsciously she thought of her own daughter and how traumatic an experience like that would be, not only for the girl but for the family as well.

"Of course," answered Ricky, now wide awake. "We'll be there as soon as we can."

She heard the click as he hung up the phone. "Is there anything I can do?" she asked.

"If you wouldn't mind, would you call folks on the east side of the valley? You're the first ones I've called over there and I need to get out and catch and saddle my mare. That will save me some time. I've already called everyone on my side."

Jessie imagined the almost 80-year-old hurrying to catch and load a horse. "I can do that," she answered.

***

She was into her second call when Ricky came

bounding down the stairs. He entered Jimmy Ray's room, turning on the light and stepping directly to the boy. He shook his shoulder. "Jimmy Ray, get up. Juan needs some help."

The 12-year-old squinted at the light. "What?"

"Get up and get dressed and go catch Pardner. We need to help look for Juanita." He patted the boy's shoulder. "Are you awake?"

"Yes, sir," answered the boy quietly as he threw the covers back and away.

"Good. We'll be outside."

Ricky then hurried through the living room where his wife was on the phone. Their eyes met and each nodded acknowledgement. Each knew what needed to be done. Taking his black felt hat from the hat rack and his coat from the hook next to the door he marched directly to the bunkhouse. He entered without knocking and flipped the light switch. "Scott, Vicente, our neighbors need some help. Get dressed quick and meet me at the barn." He stayed just long enough to see the boys roll from their beds.

At the tack room, he took a halter from the rack then strode to the horse pen. In the glow of the security light he saw Pardner, the big black standing in the corner. The horse bobbed his head then each approached the other, meeting in the middle. He rubbed the horse's forehead and patted him hard between his front legs. "We've got work to do Pardner, and I'm thinking Jimmy Ray'll want to ride you tonight." With that, he led the horse to the hitching rail outside the tack room. He heard the screen door slam at the house and knew that Jimmy Ray was on his way and within seconds the boys from the bunkhouse could be heard approaching.

Ricky caught the good looking buckskin colt and led him to the saddling area. Jimmy Ray finished brushing Pardner and handed the brush and curry comb to his dad. Scott saw and without question grabbed a halter to catch the big palomino. Vicente, though, stood waiting, not knowing what to do.

Several times since he had come to the ranch Ricky had tried to get him to ride but the boy had begged off each time. He admitted once to the boss that he was afraid of the big animals and though Ricky and Scott and tried to encourage him he wanted nothing to do with horses or riding. It had been hard for Ricky to understand, how could anyone choose not to ride, but the boy was adamant, though Ricky admitted that having someone who actually wanted to weld and fix trucks and machinery was a nice change.

Ricky studied the boy over the saddle he had just thrown on the buckskin. "Vicente, would you please start the Dodge and hook up the trailer? The key is on the pegboard in the kitchen. We'll be there in just a sec to load and go."

"Yes, *Patrón*," answered the boy respectfully. He quickly turned and paced toward the house. Ricky shook his head, wondering why Jessie couldn't seem to bring herself to see the change in the boy. The thought left as quickly as it came because there were more pressing matters. He buckled the breast collar then reached under the horse to adjust the cinch. By that time Jimmy Ray had wrestled the heavy saddle to Pardner's back so Ricky helped him finish saddling.

They heard the rattle and clatter of the big diesel as it started on the cold night. By the time Scott had the palomino saddled Vicente had the trailer hooked up. The horses were loaded and the three boys jumped into the truck while Ricky hurried to the kitchen to see Jessie in case she had more news.

She met him at the door and passed over every flashlight they had in the house. "It's a dark night. You'll need these." Obviously there was no news. "If you're not back by daylight Jewell and I will bring breakfast of some kind."

Ricky, arms cradling flashlights, leaned to kiss her

then quickly marched to the truck. Driving on the road in the dark night they could see only the lighted path to the front but noting on the side. Ricky explained what little he knew about the call for help to the curious boys and expressed his appreciation that they had rushed to get ready without waiting for an explanation. They arrived at the tiny, two-track dirt road leading to Juan's house. There were already several trucks and trailers parked on the county road and they could see flashlights shining here and there through the brush and trees close to the house.

Three hurriedly saddled cow horses stepped lively into the darkness ridden by Ricky, Jimmy Ray and Scott. Vicente walked beside. Each had a flashlight though they were not yet turned on because the bald tracks of the road were plain to see in the dim starlight.

They rode directly to the house and joined a group of horsemen leaning on their saddle horns next to men on foot listening to Alonzo, who seemed to be in charge. At his feet was the kerosene lamp casting an eerie shadow on his face. Alonzo looked directly at the newcomers. Subdued nods of greeting were exchanged. Ricky looked at the men in the group. Some were farm owners, some ranch owners, some hired hands. He knew them all. He had worked alongside many on their ranches and many had helped him at various times for roundup. He had sat next to some at the annual FFA bar-b-que and others he knew just because they all lived here together. He noticed a couple of farmers from the far north side of the valley. They had been in a squabble recently and there were rumors of lawsuits yet here they were, standing side-by-side to help find the missing girl of possibly the poorest family in the valley, and an illegal immigrant family at that. He smiled as he heard the calls for the lost girl. He gazed at the many flashlights erratically beaming this way and that by the searchers already in the brush. He loved this place and these people.

Ricky's group was assigned the area to the north of the house. All in the group scattered, shining their lights under every tree and bush.

The night wore on. More trucks and trailers arrived, more men and women, boys and girls, bundled tightly against the intensifying cold of the early morning. The area was alive with searchers and the air full of calls for the girl. Hour after hour the rescue party searched, hour after hour their searching circle expanded until it was two miles from the house. Hour after hour the despair deepened, settling thick and cold into the chests of all the volunteers, but even more deeply into the souls of Juan, Rosalinda, Alonzo and Gabriella.

Chapter 19

Vicente looked under the tree again. His flashlight was getting dim and he knew it couldn't last much longer. He pushed into the juniper tree shining the light. There was something at the base but he couldn't quite tell what it might be. The tree was dry and as he pushed into it the dry, quasi-leaves of the desert evergreen fell down his neck. He ignored the aggravation, then at last close enough he reached in to retrieve a discarded piece of cloth. It was rotted and old and had nothing to do with Juanita. He frowned in exasperation then extricated himself from the tree. He removed his coat and the snap-up western shirt to shake out the tree debris.

He looked to the east hoping to see the graying of the skyline but was disappointed. He had no watch and didn't know the time but he knew sunrise had to be approaching. He was tired and hungry but despite the discomfort, he felt good about helping. He felt needed and enjoyed the thought that he was helping someone he didn't even know. All through the long night he had crossed paths with other searchers. Their nods of acceptance made him feel like he belonged though he didn't know them and they didn't know him.

He was at least half a mile from the house and could see the lights of several people, most on foot, between where he stood and the girl's small house. He turned his light toward his face. The bulb glowed a dull orange rather than a bright white. As he watched it the wire went dark, the flashlight was completely dead.

He instantly panicked at the total darkness but as his eyes adjusted he realized that if he looked at the horizon he could at least make out the locations of the trees in the dim starlight. He wondered if perhaps additional batteries or spare flashlights might be available back at the house. Slowly, he walked that direction. He could see the trees but not the ground. Several times he tripped over brush or stray sticks. He stood to brush his pants then looked at the horizon and could see what appeared to be an opening between two trees ahead. He took two steps then the earth suddenly dropped from beneath his feet. The fall was immediate and he hit bottom face first.

He pushed to his knees, sputtering and spitting he brushed the dirt from his face. His cap was gone. He knew it had to be there to the front. He leaned forward, hands moving back and forth feeling in the dirt for the Dallas Cowboys cap with the embroidered star that Ricky had given him. His fingers felt the cloth. "There you are," he said as he reached for it. "What the heck?" It wasn't his cap but something else wrapped in cloth. He felt farther and found a shoulder, then a neck and finally a head.

He stood quickly but was careful not to step on the girl. He puckered his lips and gave a loud whistle, thankful that Raul had taught him when they were in the fourth grade. He whistled again. "Over here," he shouted. "I found her."

He could hear at least two horses loping toward him. "Where are you," came the shouts.

"Here, in a hole." He knew they were close because he could suddenly see the lights flashing through the tree above. "Right here but watch out, there's a big hole."

A horse slid to a stop at the edge spewing dust and dirt onto the boy. He covered his head and the girl as best he could. Suddenly a strong flashlight beam lit the bottom of the hole. There in a crumpled heap was Juanita with a nasty gash on her forehead. Blood had formed a line down her cheek to her neck and turned the collar of her plaid shirt a rusty brown.

Searchers came running amidst shouts of "They found her. They found her." The horseman jumped into the hole and quickly checked for anything broken. He lifted the unresponsive girl to a group of people kneeling at the side then turned to put a big hand on the boy's shoulders.

"Good work," he said then turned to take the hands of people on the bank and with their assistance, scrambled out.

***

Gabriella was out searching with everyone else when she heard Vicente's whistle and call. She sprinted that direction with her own dimming flashlight barely lighting the path. She arrived just as Juanita was being lifted from the hole. She stood at the side looking down. The scene was brightly lit with several flashlights trained on the man and boy. She saw the big cowboy, one of the hired hands from a ranch across the way, put his hand on the thin boy's shoulder and noticed the nod. She wasn't able to hear anything but it seemed obvious that the young boy must have been the finder. She wondered who he was until it dawned on her that she had seen him at Jessie's house one of the times they went to clean. She watched as the big man was helped out of the hole then as he turned back and extended his own hand. With a grunt, he lifted the boy up and out of the hole in one fluid motion.

The crowd followed as Juanita was carried to the house. Within seconds truck horns were being honked to let the faraway horsemen know the girl had been found. Gabriella's first instinct was to run to the house to be with her sister but something held her in place. She shined her dismal light toward the boy. "Are you the one that found her?" They were the only ones left at the side of the crevasse.

He nodded.

"Thank you." She then turned and ran, following the crowd to the house, not realizing she was leaving him with no light to find his way back.

She ran through the crowd gathered on the hard-packed dirt in front of the modest home. Their faces showed relief that Juanita had been found but that relief was tempered with concern because the girl was unconscious. Gabriella dashed into the house and saw her sister on the couch. Carla, the ex-nurse was there cleaning the head wound. Rosalinda sat on the edge of the couch holding her prayer beads to her chest and rocking back and forth.

Carla looked up at Gabriella's entrance and gave her a worried smile then returned to her ministrations with expert hands.

"Is she going to be okay?"

"She really should go to the hospital but your mom and dad get that worried look if I even try to suggest it. She's young and healthy, her pupils are responding and her heartbeat and respiration are good. I think she'll be fine."

Gabriella breathed a sigh of relief then patted her mother on the shoulder. The round woman looked up, weakly smiled then returned to her prayers.

***

Juan and Alonzo were thanking all the volunteers and promising their assistance in the event it might ever be needed. Men, women and children cheerily waved as cars, trucks and trailers left in a steady stream of headlights, taillights and dust. Among the few lingering stragglers were Ricky, Scott and Jimmy Ray. They sat their horses side-by-side talking to Juan. He was reiterating his thanks and telling the story of how the old truck would not start and how happy he was that Alonzo's truck had been available to call for help. At the mention of a non-running truck, Ricky sat up, looking around.

"Vicente," he called loudly.

Vicente was leaning on a fence post at the corner of the garden waiting patiently for Ricky to be finished so they could go home. After returning to the house by following a man and horse, he purposefully stayed out of sight. He'd heard several of the volunteers ask who found the girl but no one knew. He couldn't understand it but he didn't want them to know. It was enough for him to know that he had been in the right place at the right time, and it didn't hurt that the pretty girl knew and had told him thanks face-to-face. "Yes, sir," replied the boy to the call. He walked toward his boss.

"Juan says his truck is acting up. We'll rest this morning but can you come this afternoon and take a peek at it?"

"Yes, sir," he agreed with a coy smile, happy that it was hidden in the darkness. The truck was here—and so was she.

***

The saddles were returned to their stands and the horses back in the corral with a new bale of hay. Ricky leaned on the hitching rail watching the boys. At least two were so tired they could hardly keep their eyes open. He was proud of them and their willingness to answer a call for service. Scott and Jimmy Ray had gone immediately to sleep in the warmth of the truck on the way home. He had expected all three to sleep but he noticed in his rear view mirror that Vicente hadn't slept. Instead, he was quiet, simply looking out the window into the darkness.

"It's 4:30. Do you boys want breakfast or would you rather take a nap?"

"Nap for me," requested Scott, his breath blowing white in the predawn darkness. Jimmy Ray only nodded, barely able to hold his head up. Ricky waited for Vicente's answer. He got a shrug. "Then off to bed. I'll call you at 9:00."

The older boys went to the bunkhouse while Ricky

and Jimmy Ray strolled to the house. The boy shed his clothes and was asleep in his bed before Ricky had finished climbing the stairs. The rancher tried to be quiet in case Jessie was asleep but she questioned him as soon as he opened the door.

"Is she all right?"

"I think she's gonna be okay. I didn't see her but they said she had a gash on her head. Carla was there to take care of her so let's hope all is good."

Ricky slipped into the bed, pulling his wife close for the welcome warmth. "You feel so good," he whispered, then he too was asleep before she could answer.

***

Ricky barely cracked an eye when Jessie snuck out of bed at 6:00. She let Jimmy Ray sleep, no school for him today, but woke Jewell to get ready for the bus. After breakfast she woke Ricky, explaining that since Jimmy Ray was missing school Jewell didn't want to ride the bus alone so she was taking her in and would be back just after noon.

"Okay," he mumbled. Then, with a deep breath, threw the blankets off and sat up. He squinted at the silhouette of his wife standing at the door in front of the hall light. "I told the boys they could sleep till 9:00. I'll get up for chores and cook them up some breakfast of some kind." He stood while rubbing his face then walked to his wife. They embraced and kissed. "You be careful," he admonished.

"You too," she added. See you this afternoon. Love you." And with that she was out the door and he could hear her soft footfalls on the stair carpet, then, within a minute he heard the kitchen door close and they were gone.

He resisted the temptation to get back into bed though the thought was very enticing. He dressed quickly then descended the stairs and exited the house while donning his heavy wool coat. Spring was around the corner but winter was showing its reluctance to leave.

True to his word he called the boys precisely at 9:00. He grinned at the groans realizing he felt the same way.

"It'll be an easy day today, I promise," he volunteered, and he meant it. The picket fence around the cemetery needed painting so that was the plan and he had already loaded the paint and brushes into the truck.

After breakfast the rancher, two teens and a preteen walked toward the truck. Ricky noticed the Californian. "Vicente, where's your hat?"

The boy rubbed his hair subconsciously. "I lost it last night looking for the girl."

"It was pretty dark wasn't it?" commented the rancher. He glanced at each of the boys. "I'm sure glad they found her. Were any of you close by when the call came?" Jimmy Ray and Scott shook their heads while Vicente shrugged.

Ricky pointed to the house. There's an extra cap on the hat rack just inside the door. Go ahead and grab it to keep the sun off your face."

Vicente jogged to the house and returned wearing an orange cap advertising an irrigation company. All piled into the truck and were soon at the small ranch cemetery. The painters kept up a lively banter while working and as the morning progressed the sun brought the welcome warmth. It wasn't long before they shed their coats. The work was enjoyable and not strenuous. Time passed quickly and they completed the painting by early afternoon.

Ricky looked toward the horizon, remembering a windmill he wanted to check. "You boys want to go with me to check the mill at the Blazer pasture?"

Jimmy Ray and Scott quickly agreed but Vicente was hesitant.

"What's wrong?" queried the boss.

Vicente looked down at the round toed boots, new only a few weeks earlier but now scuffed and because of today's project, splattered white with paint. "I thought you wanted me to go to look at the truck for Juan Reyes."

Ricky quickly put his hand to his forehead. "Ah, you're right. I forgot. Let's go to the house and get a snack then you can see what you can find out. You can take this truck since it has all the tools. We'll check on the windmill in the jeep while you're gone."

***

Jessie casually leaned on the counter at the small elementary school office. She had brought Jewell to school that day and now that her limited shopping and errands in the tiny town were completed she wanted to check the girl out and take her home. The mother was gratified by the huge smile on her daughter's face as she came through the door. Together they walked to Jessie's Dodge truck and hopped in. In minutes they were driving on the smooth, county road toward home.

The conversation was pleasant. Jessie was enjoying her daughter more every day. The girl was getting old enough to have real talks and they were best of friends. Jessie was grinning at one of Jewel's comments when she noticed a vehicle coming toward them on the graded county road. It looked like Ricky's truck but what would it be doing here? It must be someone else. She slowed, hoping nothing was wrong but the truck kept hurrying toward them with a dust cloud billowing behind. As it grew closer and passed by she noticed Vicente driving with one hand on the wheel, one hand on the passenger seat back and an orange cap pulled low.

She shook her head. What was that all about? She frowned, slightly at first, then much more deeply at the sudden realization that he had stolen the truck and was running away. She slapped the steering wheel. "I knew it," she said in exasperation and anger.

"Knew what?" asked Jewel innocently.

Jessie recovered quickly, at least all appearances showed her calm and relaxed but inside she was seething. "Oh, nothing, she replied putting on a show of nonchalance. "Now, you were telling me about what your science teacher said." But she wasn't listening, she was getting madder every minute—mad that Ricky trusted the gangster so much. *Well, that'll teach him*, she decided.

She drove into the ranch yard, knuckles white from the tight grip on the steering wheel. She looked for her husband to tell him about the stolen truck but he was nowhere to be seen and the jeep was gone. Jewel strolled into the house while her mother looked quickly to see if anything else had been stolen. Nothing seemed missing so she went in the house to check there. The first place she looked was the drawer in the kitchen where they kept an emergency stash of money, usually a couple hundred dollars or so. It was gone!

Jessie slammed the drawer in disgust and stomped her foot, hurting it which caused her to be even angrier. She sat hard in a chair, tightly folded her arms and gritted her teeth. *Wait till he gets home*, she thought while shaking her head.

Twenty minutes later she heard the jeep roll to a stop in the driveway. She was sitting in the same position, waiting, practicing her speech. She could hear them laughing as they approached the house. Jimmy Ray burst in, laughing at something Scott had said, his young face under his black felt hat a picture of happiness.

"Hi, mom," he blurted, hardly looking at her as he raced to the living room for some reason. The big teen was next. He stopped suddenly as he looked at the woman of the house, then nodded perceptively and stepped back out the door. He bumped into Ricky, one exiting, one entering.

"What's wrong," asked the rancher to the teen.

"Nothing," I just need something from the bunkhouse." He stepped around the boss and was quickly away leaving Ricky at the door. With a puzzled expression the man watched him go for the briefest instant then he too crossed the threshold. The look on his face when he noticed her would have been comical to Jessie had she not been so angry.

164

Chapter 20

Vicente arrived at the small, cobbled together house and stood at the door of the truck for a moment. The house was about the same size as his parent's home back in LA and he nodded approval as he saw that as much as possible this homestead was well cared for. The dirt path leading from a stone archway and connected hedge fence was broomed clear of dust. No weeds lived in the dirt yard and there was one small planter box with a few dry, scraggly flowers next to the front door.

"*Hola*," he yelled from the archway where he waited to see if anyone was home.

"*Un momento, por favor,*" came the reply from the back. In a few seconds Rosalinda emerged from the back corner. When she saw him she smiled broadly showing at least two missing teeth. She spoke rapid-fire Spanish at seeing the boy, inviting him into the yard to stand under a cottonwood tree just getting spring leaves because the days were warmer even though the nights were still cold. Her graying hair was pulled sternly back in a bun which caused her face to appear round.

"How is the little one?" he asked.

Her grin expanded. She is fine, tired but fine. Did you come last night to help?"

"Yes. I was here and am so happy she was found and is

doing well. *Patrón* Ricky said your truck wouldn't start. I've come to look," he revealed.

She laughed, made some disparaging remarks about the old Ford then nodded and pointed to where it sat. He looked around, hoping for a glimpse of the pretty girl but she was nowhere to be seen so he bowed slightly out of respect then retreated to pop the hood of the multi-colored truck.

He stood on an old milk crate that he found at the side of the house and leaned into the old Ford. He was glad it was an older model and not a newer truck with computer controls. He knew he could fix these older models, no matter the problem.

Before long he had the air breather off and was tinkering with the carburetor. From his perch on the crate he wasn't quite tall enough so he climbed into the engine compartment and squeezed his body into the cracks and crevices there to get as comfortable as possible. Right away he could see two problems, a cracked vacuum hose and a stuck butterfly valve. He was concentrating so intently on the engine that he didn't hear her approach.

"Are you finding anything," she asked in Spanish.

Her sudden appearance frightened him. He jumped, hitting his head soundly on the hood. "Ouch," he cried while reaching to rub under his cap. Slowly he turned to see the girl. She looked at him quizzically and he noticed again her large, dark eyes.

"Stuck butterfly valve," he explained pointing to the carburetor opening.

She stood on the crate for a better look and as she leaned their faces were inches apart. Vicente suddenly got goosebumps and his heart was racing.

***

Ricky looked into the face of the woman he loved and could see something was terribly wrong. "Uh. Hi, Jessie," he said tentatively. He was glad the kids weren't in the kitchen.

"Hi, yourself," she replied tersely. I told you so. I tried

to tell you but you're so stubborn sometimes." Her brow was furrowed and her lips pursed.

Her eyes bored into him but he had no idea what she was so upset about. "What did you try to tell me?" he asked and the asking seemed to infuriate her all the more.

The chair scraped on the hardwood floor as she stood, tense, leaning forward as she pointed out the door. "Don't play games with me. Your truck's been stolen."

He was in shock. "My truck's been stolen? How do you know? Is Vicente all right?"

She paused, frowning for a moment before answering. "I guess he's alright but how can you be worrying about him at a time like this. Didn't you hear me? Your truck is gone and he stole the money too."

Ricky shook his head in confusion. He pulled one of the chairs from the table to sit. He pulled his eyebrows low and locked his lips in a grimace. "Slow down. What are you talking about?"

She was still standing, so mad that tears were brimming in her eyes. She stomped her foot again. "Your truck's gone. Your truck and our money."

He was having a hard time processing the information. If the truck was stolen it must have been taken somehow from Vicente while he was driving to Juan's house. *Did the thief have a gun? Is Vicente okay? Who would steal a truck in this valley?*

He reached and touched her on her hip. "The truck and money are replaceable. Where's Vicente?"

She pushed his hand away and took a step back, confusion now on her face. "Vicente has the truck bound for parts unknown. He stole it and took off just like I said he would, and he took the money from the drawer too."

Ricky carefully placed his hat upside down on the table taking some time to think. He scratched over an ear. "I took the money from the drawer and gave it to him to take to Juan to use for his daughter. Did someone steal the truck from Vicente?"

She blinked and chewed her lip. "Uh. No. I passed him going toward town. He was in your truck."

"Of course he was in my truck. He was taking it to Juan's to do some mechanic work because the old beast won't start."

She shook her head, slowly blinking her eyes. "You mean he had permission?"

"Of course he had permission. He volunteered to take a look at the old truck to help Juan out. What made you think he stole my truck?"

She put her hands over her heart at the realization of her mistake. "I... I just saw him driving it and assumed... ."

He breathed a sigh of relief. "Oh, Jessie. He didn't steal anything. I loaned it to him because it had the tools in the box."

Her shoulders slumped and she leaned on the counter as she recognized the truth. She turned to him, obviously ashamed. "I'm sorry. It's just that he was alone in your truck."

He stood quickly and held her. She seemed suddenly frail and helpless. They embraced for a long time, her face on his shoulder, her tears soaking into his shirt.

***

Gabriella sat on the old worn seat in the truck waiting on the command from the boy to turn the key and crank the engine. When the prompt came she did as instructed while looking through the gap caused by the raised hood. The truck didn't start so at his request she stopped and waited.

"Okay. Try it again," he yelled after a moment of turning this and twisting that.

She turned the key and held it while peering through the gap at his tinkering. After 15 seconds the engine sputtered, tried to run but died with a cough. She could see through the gap his expression of concentration as he fiddled with one thing then another.

"One more time," he called.

After only cranking a short time the engine caught

then ran, missing occasionally but running still the same. He turned a screw here and pushed a hose there and the motor began to sound better. He cocked is head, listening, then changed positions and listened again. Finally he stepped from the crate to listen from several places on both sides of the truck. He was standing close to her door with an expression of quiet satisfaction. He leaned back and wiping his hands with a rag nodded with a smile. "You can turn it off now."

She rested her chin on her arms as she stared at him through the open window of the old truck. She admitted to herself that he was kind of cute.

He returned her gaze with a half-smile. He didn't seem like a stranger any longer. After all, he had been the one to find Juanita and he fixed her dad's truck. She thought of standing at the hole the evening before and seeing the cowboy place a hand of appreciation and acknowledgement on this boy's shoulder. She looked at him with a sideways glance. He was suddenly intent on his toes inside the round toed boots.

"Thank you," she said quietly.

He looked up again into her quaint, partial smile. "My pleasure," he answered while nervously wiping his hands again on the rag. "I like to fix things."

"Not just the truck. Thanks for finding Juanita."

He simply shrugged and scraped the dirt with the toe of his boot. She was impressed with his humility. No bragging or trying to impress with heroic stories of how he was able to locate the girl.

"How were you able to find her?"

He glanced away, toward the mountains to the west where the sun was just beginning to descend. He chuckled reservedly. "To tell you the truth, I just fell into the same hole and there she was."

They both laughed.

"What's your name?"

"Vicente. I'm here helping *Patrón* Ricky on the ranch

for another couple of weeks. I'm from LA. What's your name?

"Gabriella," she replied and as she watched his face she felt an indescribable pleasure. She had never particularly liked her name because it sounded more Italian than Spanish but at his expression she decided she liked her name very much.

They talked comfortably for nearly an hour until they heard a truck approach. It was one of the hands from the ranch where her father worked bringing him home. After exiting and waving to the departing truck Juan walked to where the teens were visiting.

"Hello, Papa. Vicente got the truck started," she said excitedly, reverting to Spanish when talking to her father.

"*Bien, bien*," answered the thin father not much bigger than the youngster whose hand he grasped and shook vigorously.

"The truck still has some problems but it should run until I can get some parts and do some more fixing." He looked from one to the other. "That is if you'd like me to?" He too spoke in Spanish for the benefit of the older man.

Juan nodded with a smile then touched the boy on the arm. "Come to the house to rest your feet and meet my wife. Gabriella has chores to do then we will have supper."

"I didn't go to school today so my chores are already done," she quickly replied.

"E*sta bien*," he crowed while leading the way into the house.

***

Mom and Dad,
I'm coming to enjoy this place more and more. Ricky pays me for work and I've been helping on some vehicles. Thanks Dad for teaching me. I've been thinking a lot about Antonio. He would have liked it here too. I've met a lot of good people and I've met a girl. It's late so I'll tell you about her later.
Love, Vicente

***

The early morning sun streamed through the window, the rays resting on Jessie as she stood in the kitchen facing the stove cooking hotcakes with her back to her family and the two teens. She had tried to talk to the boy from LA when he walked in that morning but there just didn't seem to be anything to say. She had been remorseful at her misconception the day before and vowed to try to like the boy, but he had remained distant, only grunting answers to her question of what he wanted to eat.

Whereas she had been reluctant to engage the youngster in conversation previously because she didn't like him, now she was reluctant because of her embarrassment at the accusation to Ricky that he had stolen the truck. In unspoken agreement, they both reverted to the standard, strained silence when in each other's company.

Ricky reached for the milk to pour another glass. "Vicente, did you get Juan's truck running?"

"Yes, sir, but it has some deeper problems. I told them I'd be glad to work on it for them if they could buy the parts. I have a list for the next time you go to San Angelo though they were pretty nervous about the cost."

"I'll bet we can help some there," volunteered the ranch owner. "And speaking of money, were you able to get them to take the money we sent?"

Vicente smiled. "He made me agree that it was just a loan and he would either pay it back or work it off. He's a proud man."

Jessie turned the hotcake in the cast iron skillet thinking of the first time they met the Reyes family when they showed up and volunteered to help with the moving. "A good man," she said barely loud enough to be heard.

"Yes," agreed Ricky, "a good man." He glanced to Jessie who had turned from the stove at his comment. "I've been needing to go to San Angelo to get some vaccine for the horses anyway. Today's as good a day as any. Would you like to go with me? We can drop Jimmy Ray and Jewel at school on the way and Scott and Vicente can muck out the water tanks in the corrals. They've been anxious to get to that, haven't you boys?"

She watched Scott's face as it broke into a knowing smile.

"I know I have," he volunteered. "Counting the days. How about you, Vicente?"

She couldn't see his face because his back was to her but she heard him say, "Sounds good to me. He then looked toward Ricky and asked. "When we're finished can I go to Juan's in the jeep to check on Juanita?"

Ricky nodded while gazing at his wife. "You know you can."

***

"We'll be back in time to pick you up after school," instructed Ricky as Jimmy Ray and Jewell jumped out of the truck at the small, rural school. The couple held hands across the center console of the truck as they watched their children walk down the sidewalk and into the large covered patio which led to the classrooms. Just under the shade they separated, each turning to wave to their parents before strolling in opposite directions, Jewell to the elementary classrooms and Jimmy Ray to the Middle School.

Ricky gave Jessie's hand a squeeze, then put the truck in drive and eased away from the curb. "We'd best be heading out so we can make it back in time so they won't have to ride the bus and be alone with the boys at the ranch."

Jessie gazed at her hands on her lap, quiet until they were on the paved road leading toward San Angelo. She rubbed her left thumb with her right. After several minutes of silence she gazed at her husband. "I'm sorry about yesterday. I shouldn't have jumped to conclusions." She turned to watch the scenery as it passed by out the window, all the while chewing on her lip.

Ricky reached to touch her shoulder. At his touch she turned. He smiled and was rewarded with a small smile in return.

"It's okay. I can see how you could think he stole the truck. He's doing well and is a good boy. In time I think you'll come to see that."

The corners of her mouth turned down as she returned to the scenery out the window. "Maybe so," she replied with a sigh. "But I just don't like him. I don't know, maybe it's a personality thing." She turned to make eye contact. "I'll promise you this, though. I'll be nice to him for the rest of the time he's here."

Ricky smiled. "That's all anybody could ask. Thanks."

Chapter 21

Vicente slowed the jeep in response to the flashing lights of the school bus coming in the opposite direction. He stopped at the little two-track road leading from the county road to the small, two-bedroom home. The bus stopped also to allow Gabriella to exit and walk in front, then with a roar and a cloud of dust it passed the jeep on its way to other homes farther from town.

Gabriella stopped for a moment, intently studying the jeep then smiled as she recognized the young man in the driver's seat. She stood, arms folded over a school book held at her chest as he pulled forward onto the small road.

"Hi," she greeted.

"Hi to you too," he responded. "I came to check on Juanita. Would you like a ride to the house?"

"That's so nice of you on both counts. Juanita is doing good and I'd love a ride." She quickly walked around the jeep and slipped into the passenger seat. With the book on her lap she ran her hands under her long hair and lifted it away from her face and neck to rest attractively at her back.

Vicente smiled at the sight then engaged the clutch and started down the road. In the three minutes it took to get to the house they eased comfortably into a conversation just as they had the evening before. At the house he coasted the jeep to a stop amongst the flailing and scattering chickens in the yard then killed the motor. They sat for two hours visiting about everything under the sun until Gabriella mentioned that she had chores to do so together they continued their conversation while he helped.

He had never known a girl so easy to talk to, and so smart too. It seemed like no matter what the topic was she knew something about it. Not in a know-it-all way but in a matter-of-fact way. The more he was around her the more smitten he was. He decided that if this is what love felt like then he was all for it.

***

The sun was disappearing behind the mountains when old, multi-colored Ford truck pulled into the yard to park next to the jeep just as the teens were finishing chores for the day. Juan waved them over and expressed appreciation for the mechanic work Vicente had done on his old truck. "Come into the house for supper," he instructed.

The family and their guest sat around the rickety table joined this night by Juanita who was well enough to be up and around. Vicente ate as much as he had the evening before. The food was spectacular once again, authentic and home-made. He hadn't realized how much he had missed his mother's cooking. With a wry smile, he thought of the Mexican dishes Jessie had fixed. They were tolerable but obviously lacking in authenticity. He thought of home and was suddenly anxious to return. Not to the gang or even the neighborhood, but to see his parents. To tell them of the things he had learned and, if they would accept it, to apologize for the heartache he had caused.

"Do you go to college?" Rosalinda asked out of the blue.

It took him a moment to realize that the question had been directed at him. He glanced from the questioner to Gabriella. She was studying her plate and he wondered why the question had made her uncomfortable. He turned his gaze back to Rosalinda. He sadly shook his head while answering, "No, Mother. My life took another path after high school."

The Matriarch patted Gabriella's arm. "Gabriella wants to go to college but can't."

He studied her again. Her shoulders were slumped and her head hung and she was obviously uncomfortable. The wooden chair scraped on the concrete floor as she pushed from the table then stood to begin clearing dishes. At her movement, everyone else did the same effectively ending any conversation about college.

Vicente thanked his hosts then stepped through the door toward the jeep. He was excited as Gabriella accompanied him. They stopped, both leaning on the jeep, arms folded against the night chill.

"Thank you for stopping by and helping today," she said in English.

He tried his best to study her face in the dim light. "My pleasure. I'm glad that Juanita is up and around." He paused then asked the question that had been nagging him since supper. "Why can't you go to college?"

Her exasperation was evident in her sigh and she paused for a full minute before speaking. He waited. Finally, she asked, "Are you legal?"

He was surprised at the question and frowned. "Of course I'm legal. Aren't you?" He saw her shiver at the cold and wished he had a jacket he could lend. Then he was shocked at her answer.

"No. I was born in Mexico but came here as a baby."

He thought for a moment before asking, "What difference does that make?"

She stared unseeing into the distance and he realized that perhaps the shiver may have been caused by more than the cold. She looked at the ground, her head was down and her long hair hung down each side of her face.

At length, she answered, "We can't afford the tuition to begin with and Texas makes illegals pay out-of-state tuition too."

Vicente shook his head. He knew the smart kids in his

school, many of whom were very poor, and at least two that he knew were illegal, had been able to get scholarships to attend college. He thought back to his high school days and the assemblies the school put on to encourage college attendance. At that time his interest in college was non-existent but he could remember his high school counselor extolling the virtues of community colleges in California and their inexpensive tuition for legal and even illegal residents. "Can't you apply for scholarships?" he asked, sure that a girl as smart as she could get one.

In the dim light he saw her shake her head, the long hair waving as it fell on both sides of her face. "I don't dare do anything that would draw attention to my family." She pushed from the jeep and turned to face him. "Thanks again for coming. I have some homework to do."

He pushed from his leaning on the jeep wishing she would stay and talk. "Can't you do your homework later?"

She shook her head, touched his arm and with a "Goodnight," turned to dejectedly shuffle with head down back into the house. He watched her go wishing there was something he could do.

The drive back to the ranch was cold in the open topped jeep but he hardly noticed. He was thinking of Gabriella and wondering if there might be a chance she could attend college back in LA where it was less expensive and they didn't care if a student was illegal.

***

Jessie heard the jeep pull into the driveway and stop. She was alone in the kitchen. Jewell had gone to bed and Ricky, Scott and Jimmy Ray were watching an old John Wayne movie in the living room. She stood to look out the window at the young man. He sat in the jeep for a time before getting out and walking through the halo of brightness from the security light at the horse corral. Her dislike for him lay heavy on her shoulders. *Darn him. Why did he have to be so stubborn?* she wondered to herself. She had tried to like him but just couldn't. She was glad, she supposed, that Ricky and Vicente had come to terms but she secretly was anxious for the California boy to return to where he came from. She thought of Scott and acknowledged her love for the big teen. She was comfortable with him staying as long as he liked. She frowned at the comparison. Scott was always so willing to please, so quick to compliment and anxious to do whatever was asked of him. Vicente, on the other hand, well, he was just Vicente. She turned from the window to sit again at the table and reminded herself that she had promised to be nice to the boy until he went home.

***

The bunkhouse was dark as Vicente approached. It was too early for Scott to be in bed so, Vicente decided, he must be in the house with Ricky's family. All the better, he thought. He wanted so alone time anyway. He opened the door, grateful for the warmth of the room then flipped the light switch. He strode directly to a small writing desk next to his bed and extracted a pen and paper from the drawer. Forty minutes later he sealed the letter into the envelope, attached a stamp then stood and stretched before looking out the window toward the lights at the ranch house.

At the looking, he thought of Ricky and his time in Texas and was ashamed at the way he had acted. He was thankful for what he had learned on the ranch and he was determined to make things right with his parents. The letter on the desk was the first step. Maybe another week then he would ask the boss soon if he could call his parents to ask them if he could return home.

Picking up the letter he tapped it against the palm of his hand. Stepping toward the door he took his coat from the hook and pulled it on. With a spring to his step he strolled past the horse corral onto the ranch road leading to the County road and the mailbox, thinking on the way of his family, Ricky's family, Scott, and most of all, about Gabriella. He admitted that he hardly knew her yet in the same thought, realized that he liked her a lot. Wouldn't it be grand if she could somehow go to LA to go to school?

He placed the letter in the mailbox and lifted the red flag indicating outgoing mail. With a smile he tapped the old metal box lightly then turned to stroll the quarter mile back to the bunkhouse.

***

Vicente timed his afternoon drive to the Reyes house so he could pick up Gabriella and Juanita from the school bus to give them a ride. Each afternoon for the next week he and Gabriella visited while he tinkered on the truck, adding the belts and a heater hose that Ricky and Jessie had bought in San Angelo. If he had wanted, Vicente could have finished the entire job in a single afternoon but he drew the project out as long as possible. After an hour each day of mechanic work the youngsters did chores together and every evening he was invited to stay for supper. It was a happy week.

On Friday afternoon they went for a walk away from the house. For the first time they held hands as they walked.

***

Ricky went out to feed the horses. The early, Saturday morning sun slowly warmed his back as he leaned on the rails of the horse pen and watched the horses eat. He, Jimmy Ray and Scott would ride through the cows today. Most already had calves on the ground but there were a few stragglers so they would be checking for any that might be having trouble calving. He realized that meant leaving Vicente at the ranch with Jessie and Jewell. The plan was for the boy to finish some welding on the corrals to keep him busy.

He had made that suggestion to Jessie before he left the house that morning. Though she agreed, he could see that she continued to be less than excited at the prospect.

"You can stay in the house and keep the doors locked if it makes you feel better," he had suggested.

She agreed then brightened considerably. "Today is the first Saturday of March. That means Rosalinda and the girls will come to help clean. They'll be here till nearly noon and you'll be back not much after. I know you trust him and I guess based on your trust that I trust him too. Still, I'll feel better if we're not here alone."

He turned at the sound of Scott and Vicente's footsteps approaching.

"Howdy Boys. Let's go in for breakfast then we've got work to do today." The threesome turned to walk toward the house. "Vicente?"

The youngster looked up at the ranchman, waiting.

"Scott, Jimmy Ray and I'll be riding today. Can you stay and finish the welding on the corrals?"

The grin was telling for Ricky. It seemed to say two things. First, that he was glad to be entrusted with a job and second, thankfulness that he was not being asked to ride. Ricky grinned at the thought.

"Yes, sir," the boy answered immediately.

After breakfast, Vicente stood at the welding machine watching three cowboys on three good cowhorses ride up a hill leading to one of the ranch pastures. As they disappeared into the distance he started the welding machine, donned a leather welding jacket and stuffed a handful of welding rods into his back pocket.

Two hours later, his supply of welding rod depleted, he retreated to the workshop to get a new supply. Just before he stepped in he heard a vehicle approach. He stood at the door and smiled as he saw Juan's old Ford come into view, bouncing over the ruts in the road. He smiled smugly at the sound of the engine running smoothly. Through the glare of the sun on the windshield he could see three occupants. As the truck stopped he happily saw that Gabriella was one of the passengers. She stepped from the truck and stared his direction, then with a bright smile, waved before turning toward the house with her mother and sister.

***

Jewell and Juanita climbed the stairs to play on the

landing in front of the upstairs bedroom and bathroom while the three women cleaned the house. Rosalinda, knowing her way around from years of cleaning marched directly to the small closet where the vacuum cleaner was stored. She flipped on the light, grabbed the vacuum handle with one hand and the long cord with the other. She hooked the bottom of the door with her heel and slammed the door shut, not realizing that she had neglected to turn off the light.

For nearly two hours the ladies cleaned, then at Jessie's insistence, sat around the kitchen table eating bread and honey. They talked of neighbors and friends, of Juanita's harrowing experience, of Ricky's hired hand fixing their truck and of anything else that naturally came up in conversation. Finally, at noon, Rosalinda stood and called to the interior of the house, "Juanita, *vámonos*! Let's go."

The girl skipped down the stairs, begged for one piece of bread and honey then the three walked to the truck and were gone.

Jessie waved from the back porch as she watched them go. After the truck was gone from sight she noticed the throbbing hum of the welding machine in the corrals. She could see Vicente at the far side welding on the pipe. Good, she thought. *You stay busy out there and we'll stay in the house.*

Turning back inside she noticed that the vacuum was still out. She started taking it back to the closet but stopped, fingering the dangerous looking, fraying cord. She would leave it out for Ricky to fix at his first opportunity.

Chapter 22

The ranch house had been remodeled several times, most recently a couple of years after Ricky and Jessie moved in with their family. It had been built in the 1950s though in the course of the various remodels much of the older parts of the house had been replaced. The small vacuum cleaner closet was a holdout. The original wood, insulation and wiring had never been replaced and from all outward appearances, the material was still sound and functional. From the inside though, the electrical wiring was flawed.

It had been years since the light to the closet had been left on for an extended period of time. Today, though it had only been three hours, the heat from the electricity was building like a slow moving, faraway thunderstorm. Completely unnoticed, the first tendril of smoke escaped from the dry wood immediately above the wall switch into which the electric wiring was stapled. In fact, it was the staple that had caused damage to the cable which caused the buildup of the heat. The tiniest of flames appeared, licking at the board, growing ever so slowly, aided by the increasing heat of the wiring. In an instant flash of sparks the wiring arced one last time before the circuit breaker opened, but the sparking only caused the small but growing fire to increase. Climbing upward along the board, the fire, no longer relying on the electrical system, built slowly in intensity, held in check temporarily by the lack of oxygen until it burned through the thin, wooden wall covering on the inside of the closet. Once in the open, the flames reached greedily toward the ceiling, dancing on their upward trek in search of combustible materials. At the ceiling they found much to burn. The fire spread upward and outward with surprising thoroughness and swiftness, engulfing the closet interior, sucking available oxygen from the gap under the door, searching with a mind of its own for an escape from the confines of the four walls.

***

Jessie looked out the window toward the pasture, anxious for the return of her husband. Seeing no one coming from that direction she glanced to make sure Vicente was still working at the far side of the corrals. Satisfied that he was she called to the second-floor landing. "Jewell, Honey, I need some fresh air. I'm going to walk to check the mail. The breeze is blowing and it's a little dusty so you probably should stay in the house."

Jewell looked through her parent's bedroom. Seeing the trees slightly bending in the breeze she returned to lean on the banister, looking down at her mother. "Okay."

Jessie nodded, impressed at how accepting her daughter was of her damaged lungs and wishing for the thousandth time that it wasn't so. "Okay, I won't be gone long and I'll lock the door when I leave. We'll have lunch when I get back."

With that, she pulled on her sweater, locked and pulled the door closed then strolled through the yard onto the road.

***

Within minutes the fire had burned through the back wall of the small closet, finding a seemingly unlimited supply of oxygen and combustible materials in an unused storage room at the back of the house under Ricky and Jessie's bedroom. It raced along the walls, lapping at the ceiling, taking every advantage to grow and consume everything in its path.

Jewell, oblivious to the sudden danger, lounged on an oversized pillow on the stair landing pretending she was at a royal tea party. With her back to the banister rails, she propped her dolls around her and spoke to them in her best Old English accent as she poured imaginary tea and served the most delectable imaginary cookies.

The fire, burning in earnest in the back room suddenly broke through the wooden door at the front of the closet which allowed it access to the interior of the house. The super-heated air rushed outward and upward, causing almost immediate combustion of materials in the living room. Jewell jumped at the sudden roar, the smell of the smoke and the ear piercing screeching of the smoke alarm, then stared in horror at the rapidly growing fire immediately under the stairs.

Jumping to her feet her first thought was that she could escape to the balcony of her parent's room. She ran four steps to the door which she hastily opened amidst the first spasms of coughing from the increasing smoke. As the door opened inward the fire, a monster in its own right, hungrily sucked the new oxygen which caused the flames to swell and push explosively toward the terrified girl. She was knocked from her feet back onto the landing, her hair and eyebrows singed. She rolled to her feet, screaming in between the ever increasing coughs. Her eyes burned from the smoke and her lungs felt as though they were on fire.

She searched for any viable escape but the only option was down the stairs and through the hall at the side of the living room. The panic drove her footsteps down the stairs but a coughing fit caused her to fall and roll painfully to the bottom. She couldn't move for the coughing, all she could do was curl into a ball on the hardwood floor with her hands over her head while the ever increasing fire raged at the back of the house as well as under the stairs and in the living room to her side.

***

Jessie leaned on the window of the car chatting amiably with the mail carrier. They talked of neighbors and friends, of rain and of the coming spring. They were friends and Jessie enjoyed the opportunity to visit, especially since she stayed at home most days and only talked to her family and occasionally to Scott.

***

Vicente finished the last weld with a grunt of satisfaction. Taking off the welding jacket and hood he hung them carefully on the hooks of the welding trailer then stepped behind to kill the motor. He wiped his brow with his sleeve as the motor growled to a stop. The silence was welcome though it took him a moment to realize that all was not silent. He turned at the roar coming from the direction of the house and froze in instant shock. The flames were leaping from the roof, climbing into the sky amidst thick, dark clouds of smoke. In a microsecond, with horrifying realization and perfect clarity, he recalled his second day at the ranch, the day he had climbed through the girl's bedroom window and with evil intent, fixed the kitchen light so it would start a fire to burn the house down. His instant, yet erroneous guilt was paralyzing for the blink of an eye. The fire was not of his causing but he couldn't know that.

His heart pounded in his chest. "Nooooo!" he screamed.

Faster than he had ever run, he now ran toward the house, climbing the corral fence that stood in his way and with youthful agility dropping to the ground to race to the house at a full sprint. Searching from side to side he hoped to see Jessie and Jewell safely out but his panic increased as he saw no sign of either.

His boots skidded to a stop, sliding on the concrete in front of the kitchen door. He reached for the knob but the door was locked. Not wasting any time he turned his back then viciously slammed his shoulder and arm into the wooden frame holding the triangle pieces of glass that made up the door window. The wood splintered, the glass shattered, and so did his elbow. The pain was almost more than he could bear. In agony he momentarily dropped to a knee, holding his elbow but in the same instant was up, reaching through the new opening with his left hand to unlock the door from the inside.

The smoke billowed out the door and was so thick on the inside that he dropped to his knees and crawled, two-legged and one-armed into the kitchen. He noticed that the flames were racing along the ceiling though at least in the kitchen the walls were not yet afire. The living room was a different story. Most of the walls were also burning and he had to sink lower and lower in attempts to breathe the less smoky air.

"Jessie, Jewell," he screamed and waited in hopeful anticipation for a response. There was none.

A large chunk of burning ceiling fell, hitting him at his shoulders. Some of the material bounded off and landed in a burning heap but a portion, burning and insanely hot, clung to his back, incinerating much of his thin shirt and burning at once into the flesh of his back and neck. He cried in agony and tried in vain to shake the embers away. The heat was tremendous and he knew he must escape or he would be caught in the inferno. Turning in resigned hopelessness he started his retreat to the kitchen and safety in the yard when he heard coughing, loud and harsh, coming from the interior. Without thought for his own pain and with renewed realization and utter shame that he had caused the fire, he crawled as quickly as possible toward the sound. The smoke was so thick he couldn't see the flames but he felt the searing, oppressive heat.

Crawling past one of the rocking chairs in the living room his hand felt a throw rug. Instinctively he grabbed it and pushed it along as he approached the foot of the stairs. To his surprise the smoke was less thick but the flames were more intense, burning three of the four walls and the entire ceiling. He stopped to listen for the coughing but heard nothing more than the overpowering sounds of the burning house.

More embers were dropping from the ceiling. They landed on and around him and as he began crawling again to where he hoped the girl was the coals imbedded themselves into his hand and knees. With abject determination he fought through the pain, crawling and calling through his own coughs, all the while hoping against hope for a sign.

He turned his head at a sound and saw through the thick haze, Jewell curled at the foot of the stairs. He noticed immediately that the wall and ceiling above her were aflame but she was in a pocket of sorts with no fire. She coughed again and he prayed they could get out.

***

Jessie stood for a moment and watched the mail carrier drive away then thumbing through the mail while walking she started the quarter mile return trip to the house. Out of habit she glanced over the tops of the Juniper trees toward her home. She blinked at the smoke rising in billows and screamed in immediate panic at the thought of Jewell alone in the house.

***

Vicente rolled the coughing girl into the rug. It was difficult because he could only use his good arm. The stairs to his immediate right were now burning as was the wall to his front. He had gotten to Jewell in the nick of time but he knew he was far from any type of safety. The small air space at the floor had disappeared and the smoke mixed with the air seared his lungs. Jewell's coughing had subsided slightly because she was now breathing through the rug which afforded some filtration. The heat was unbearable, the ceiling and walls were completely engulfed in flames and even though he was close to the floor he could feel his hair and skin burning.

With resolution born from knowing he had caused the fire, he endured excruciating pain as he forced his broken elbow to function as he pulled the girl into his arms. He knew he didn't have time to drag her so he took two breaths, coughing in between, then stood and ran through the living room into the kitchen. The standing brought him in direct contact with the flames hovering just feet from the floor. By the time he got to the kitchen his ears and the skin on his face began to burn and melt away and his shirt back was on fire. Still, he gripped the unmoving child in his arms and ran.

At the kitchen he bumped into the wall. The coals of the wood burned into his arm like a branding iron, his flesh searing and sizzling at the touch but he was beyond feeling. His brain had somehow stopped the pain and all he could think about was reaching the outer door. He took a step back to recover from hitting the wall when a burning beam from above broke, swinging down in an arc to hit him squarely in the back. He went to his knees to the burning floor but couldn't feel a thing. Pushing up he stumbled into the kitchen and out the door. He almost fell but somehow retained his balance until away from the house at the sandy driveway closer to the horse corrals. He fell to his knees, jarring his entire body. Slowly, not realizing his shirt and pants were on fire, he carefully pulled the loose end of the smoldering rug which unrolled Jewell onto the sand. Through burned and scarred eyes he noticed Jessie running toward them. It was then that his muscles lost their strength and he fell limply on his back to the sand which extinguished the flames on his clothes.

***

Jessie screamed as she saw the burning figure stumble from the house and go to his knees in the driveway. She recognized Jewell as the girl was unrolled from the rug and her heart leapt as she saw her daughter curl into a ball and continue to cough. She was alive! She raced to Jewell's side, kneeling, panting in fear and exertion, between the girl and the blackened and burned boy. She stared with dismay at the singed hair and eyebrows of her daughter and was

188

temporarily relieved as a quick inspection showed no other outward signs of damage. Jewell's coughing continued but seemed less severe as her lungs filled with clean air.

The ranch woman turned her attention to Vicente and cringed at the sight. He seemed to be gazing at her. He had no hair and his face was almost non-existent, having been burned beyond recognition. She was surprised when he raised his arm toward her.

His weak, wheezy voice was gravely and barely audible. "I'm so sorry."

Faster than time could be measured the gratitude she felt for this young man intensified a thousand fold. He had saved her little girl. This boy, the one she had hated so, had saved her precious daughter. She touched his blackened and blistered arm and at the touch felt extreme remorse at the way she had treated him. "No," she whispered. "It was me. I'm sorry."

His arm fell back to the sand, his endurance past the point of no return. She had been trained as a nurse but had never seen a burn victim with such severe injuries. If only she could call for an air ambulance. She looked dejectedly toward the house, fully engulfed in flames. She felt the heat even at this distance and knew there was no way to call. Suddenly she remembered the phone they had installed in the barn. If she hurried perhaps it might still be working. Leaping to her feet she sprinted past the horse corral to the tack room.

When she returned Jewell was coughing only sporadically so Jessie moved her to sit in the shade. There were some blisters forming on her hands and face and the sun on them was painful. Jessie returned to Vicente, shaking her head at the severity of the damage. She dared not move him so she fashioned a shade of sorts from saddle blankets from the tack room. There was no clean cloth for cold compresses so she ripped the bottom of her blouse and soaked it with the hose at the barn. She dribbled water into his mouth and fought the urge to vomit. Ever so lightly she attempted to pat his brow for some comfort but as the dead, burned skin sluffed away from his skull she could hold it no longer. Turning to the side she vomited into the sand.

When she turned back to him she was amazed that he was trying to speak. She leaned close to hear the whisper. "I'm so sorry. It was my fault," he repeated several times.

She sat on the sand at his side and lovingly touched his throat and chest, the only place on his thin body that seemed unburned, obviously protected by the rug with the girl inside that he held so tightly to his torso during the escape from the house.

As she knelt at his side she wept at his pain and at his sacrifice. She wept out of gratitude that her little girl was safe. She wept at the shame she felt for how she had treated the boy and finally she wept because she knew his chances of survival were slim at best. She prayed that somehow his suffering would cease.

Chapter 23

Over the next minutes Jessie alternated taking care of Jewell and trying to reassure her. She also did what she could to attend to the horribly burned Vicente. She dripped water from the cloth into his mouth, searching the entire time for the helicopter that she prayed would be there shortly. She glanced skyward as she heard the beating of the helicopter rotors.

In less than a minute the craft had landed in a wide, devoid of trees area thirty yards from where she stood. The paramedic, carrying a heavy medic bag jumped out before the runners had touched the ground and hurried to render aid, but he stopped short as he looked under the makeshift tent and saw Vicente lying on the sand. The flight nurse ran to his side and stopped also. Both stared for an instant at the sickening sight, then rushed into action, doing all they could to keep the boy alive.

Jessie retreated to her daughter and held her closely while watching the responders carefully load Vicente onto a gurney. The sand wouldn't allow it to roll so with Jessie's help they mostly carried it to the waiting chopper. The young mother stood away and discouragingly waved as the doors were closed. The engine noise was deafening as the helicopter rotors increased speed and the aircraft clawed the air, taking off in an almost backward ascent, then it quickly spun then angled forward and left in a rush. Jessie held her arms covering her face and ears, then as the wind decreased watched it as the reverberating whomp, whomp, whomp receded in the distance. Suddenly she could hear Ricky screaming from behind. She turned to see him riding up on the buckskin colt at a hard sprint. The horse slid on its haunches and Ricky dismounted before the horse came to a stop.

He stepped to her front and grabbed her shoulders. "Where's Jewell?" he screamed again.

Jessie wrapped her arms around his neck and held tightly, burying her face into his chest. He pushed her away enough so she could talk. "Is it Jewell?" he yelled with no sense of composure.

She shook her head then pointed with her nose to the tree where their daughter was resting. Ricky barely had time to notice the girl before his wife fell to her knees in the sand. He joined her there and held her close.

"It's Vicente," she wailed, the tears flowing freely down her cheeks.

Scott and Jimmy Ray rode onto the scene at a high lope. Ricky picked Jessie up and carried her to his truck parked near the barn. Over his shoulder he gave instructions. "Jimmy Ray, tie the horses up then come get in the truck. Scott, carry Jewell to the truck. We're going to San Angelo. Will you please stay here and take care of things till we get back. You can stay in the bunkhouse."

***

Ricky drove his Dodge truck faster than he should have all the way their little valley town. On the way Jessie took the time to more closely examine Jewell and happily found that other than singed eyebrows and eyelashes and painful but non-life threatening blisters from the burns on her forehead and arms there was no other physical damage. Emotionally, though, she was still concerned at the possible effects of the traumatic experience. They sat in the back seat, mother holding tightly to her daughter who continued to breathe harshly and cough more than occasionally.

Ricky quizzed them and after getting from Jessie and Jewell a short version of what had happened, he pulled the cell phone from his hip and dialed Román. When the phone was answered he wasted no time on pleasantries, this just wasn't the time.

"Román, I've got bad news. Our house burned. Jewell was trapped inside. Vicente went in and saved her but has been burned bad, real bad. He was airlifted out and we're on our way to the hospital in San Angelo."

Jessie quickly sat up straight. "They're taking him to Lubbock."

Ricky studied his wife over the seat. "What?"

"I just remembered, they said they were taking him to the burn center in Lubbock."

He returned his attention to the road and spoke into the phone, "Going to Lubbock. Can you get his parents there? Things don't look good."

There was a pause on the phone then Román spoke, "Of course. I'll call them now and get them on a plane."

Ricky was thankful that Román hadn't asked any more questions because he quite simply didn't have the answers.

Jewell had finally fallen asleep on her mother's arm and Jimmy Ray was also asleep in the front seat. Jessie cleared her throat and carefully not to wake her daughter, reached her hand toward the front seat. Ricky noticed and took her hand.

"I'm sorry. I should have been in the house instead of walking to get the mail. If I had only been there he wouldn't have had to go in after her."

"It wasn't your fault. Don't even think that way. What's done is done and we can't change it, we can only work through whatever does happen."

"He was burned so badly. What will his parents say?"

Ricky squeezed her hand and shook his head. "I don't know. I've been thinking about that and about how we'll pay for all this. Workman's Comp should cover the doctor bills and our house insurance should build us a new house.

The question now is Vicente and his folks. I suppose they could sue us."

Jessie gasped. She hadn't been thinking about any of those possible outcomes, she had been thinking only of Vicente. "Surely not. It was an accident."

***

Two hours into the drive they were thirty minutes from Lubbock. Jessie borrowed Ricky's phone and searched for a burn center there. She found the listing and read it silently. At last she looked to her husband. "It's called the Harnar Burn Center at UMC. It's the best in West Texas." She dropped her head and absently rubbed the black stains on her ripped blouse. The stains were left where she rubbed her fingers after she touched Vicente's arm. She shuddered involuntarily. "I hope they can do something." Ricky read her body language and noted the sigh of resignation. He reached over the seat back. They grasped hands and he gave her a loving squeeze.

The phone rang and vibrated in her hand. She jumped then passed it to Ricky when she saw the caller ID.

"Hello, Román," answered the grim-faced driver.

"Hi, Ricky. Vicente's mom and dad just got on the plane. They will be there in about two hours. I'm driving now already half way there so I'll pick them up and take them to the hospital. Are you almost there?"

"About thirty minutes. The burn center is at UMC. We're going straight there."

***

The family of four exited the truck and pausing at the sight, looked up at the sprawling, six-story hospital with the sunlight of the rapidly approaching sunset reflecting off the windows. Jessie held tightly to Ricky's hand on one side and Jewell's hand on the other, then with dread at what they would learn, followed her husband's lead through the paved parking lot and into the main lobby. Accompanied by the jingle jangle of Ricky's spurs on the hardwood floor, the family approached the front desk. They all noticed the gasp of the receptionist at the sight of Jessie's blackened and ripped blouse and Jewell's singed hair and burned face.

For the briefest instant Jessie was self-conscious at her appearance but that was short lived as the lady across the desk stood, pointed in obvious compassion and said, "The emergency entrance is at the side."

Ricky quickly answered, "Thanks, but we don't need the emergency room. Can you tell us where the burn center is? A friend of ours was flown here a couple of hours ago and we need to see how he is."

She tore her eyes from Jewell and with a nod pointed down a hall with instructions to watch for the signs that would take them there.

"Thanks," called Ricky.

At the burn center desk the receptionist quickly called for a nurse to attend to the obviously burned Jewell. The father and mother were happy for the care and waited patiently as questions were asked and ointment was applied to her face and arms.

"That should fix you up. You'll be good as new before you know it."

Jewell, with no eyebrows or eye lashes bravely smiled and the nurse looked up into Ricky's face. "We typically see much worse burns here than that. I'm glad you brought her in but there is really nothing more we can do for her here."

"Actually," he said with a frown, "we've come to see our friend. He was burned badly and was airlifted here."

"When was that?" she asked quickly.

"A couple of hours ago. Can you tell us anything?"

The look on her face told them more than they wanted to know. "I'll get Dr. Ruiz." She turned and left with a frown of her own.

Dr. Ruiz, a portly young doctor with thinning hair and bushy eyebrows came toward them from the hall. He extended his hand to Ricky while looking over the young family. His eyes lingered on Jewell and the burns. He knelt and held under her chin, turning her face from side to side.

Satisfied that what had been done was appropriate he stood to face Ricky.

"Maxine said you are asking about a patient that was flown in this afternoon?"

"Yes. His name is Vicente, about 20, about 5'8" and thin. He saved Jewell." Ricky pointed to his daughter.

Dr. Ruiz sighed. "A patient did arrive about two hours ago with third and fourth-degree burns over 80% of his body. We don't know his name or anything else about him but if it's the same person we need to talk to his parents. Do you know them?"

The cowboy nodded. "They'll be here in a couple of hours. They're flying from LA. Is there anything we can do? Can we see him?"

Dr. Ruiz glanced down the hall from which he had come. With a deep breath he once again studied the family. "He's in a medically-induced coma and wrapped from head to foot. There's not much for you to see or do."

Jessie stepped forward and waited until the doctor focused on her. "Can I sit with him for just a little while?"

The doctor looked at her ripped and blackened blouse then to Jewell once again and she could see in his eyes that he had guessed what had happened.

"Please," she added.

He stepped back then with a nod and wave invited her to follow him down the hall to the boy's room. She sat in a leather chair and hung her head at the sight. The boy was indeed wrapped from head to foot and the only movement was a slow, slight raising and falling of his chest. The monitor at his side showed heartbeat and respiration and tubes and wires crisscrossed his thin body. The air conditioning and the aroma of salves and ointments could not eliminate the sickening smell of burnt flesh.

She sat alone with him, constantly praying that he would somehow survive and be whole again though she knew that the severity of the burns was past extreme. At length, she stood and with tears in her eyes, leaned close and whispered, "Thanks for saving Jewell. I'm sorry I treated you badly. I was wrong from the start. You're a good boy and you deserved better. Please forgive me." Then, after a pause pleaded again, "Somehow, please forgive me."

She sunk into the chair and sobbed.

***

Vicente's mother and father sat side-by-side, holding hands in quiet desperation toward the back of the airplane. A well-dressed man in the window seat closed his novel and stretched his hands above his head then turned to the couple. "Do y'all live in Lubbock?" he asked with a pronounced Texas drawl.

Both shook their heads and frowned. The husband answered, "No. We live in LA. We got a call a couple of hours ago that our son was burned badly on the ranch where he was working and was being flown to Lubbock to the burn center there. We caught the first flight."

The man grimaced. "I'm sorry to hear that. Those kinds of calls are the worst. I got one one time. My daughter was in a car wreck in Pittsburgh." He shook his head as he pulled his billfold from his coat pocket and extracted a card. "I'm from Lubbock. If there is anything I can do you give me a holler. Hear?" He took his pen and scratched his home phone number on the back of the card.

Sylvia took the offered card, absently rubbing the raised lettering indicating the man's name, Quinton Calloway, Attorney at Law. She glanced into his face, confused. "We don't need a lawyer."

The man blinked quickly then with an embarrassed expression looked from wife to husband and back again. "Please forgive me. I was not offering legal help and I'm certainly not an ambulance chaser. I'm ashamed if you thought I was. The offer to help was just that, an offer to help. I've been in your shoes so I thought perhaps you might need a ride to the hospital or something."

Sylvia hung her head, humbled at the offer from a stranger and decided if all Texans were like this man she could see why Vicente loved it there.

Chapter 24

Ricky, accompanied by a nurse, peeked into the room. After a lingering gaze at the boy he said, "Honey, the kids are tired and hungry. Let's go get a motel and a shower then get a bite to eat so we can be back when his parents get here." He held is hand for her to take.

She stood, took the offered hand and wiping the tears with her free hand let him lead her from the room. In the lobby she hugged her son and daughter then followed them down the hall, out the door and to the truck.

On the way they stopped at a Wal-Mart to buy clean clothes and it was completely dark by the time they got to a motel for a shower and a short rest. When an hour had gone by they had eaten and were parking in the hospital parking lot for the second time that day.

Ricky's phone rang. He looked quickly at the caller ID then answered, "Hi, Román." After listening for only a few seconds he added. "Good. We'll meet you at the front door to the hospital."

He pushed the disconnect button and turned to Jessie. "They're parking now too and will be at the front doors in just a few minutes. Let's go."

She didn't reach for the door handle, instead, she reached for his hand and searched his face. "What if he dies?"

He shrugged. "We'll just have to wait and see. Let's go

meet them."
***

Sylvia, Vicente's mother, held tightly to her husband as they walked next to Román toward the front doors of the hospital. Her emotions were running high and she felt as though she might collapse any moment. She thought of her son and wondered for the hundredth time how bad it really was. With all her willpower she vowed to be strong. As they rounded a bend in the sidewalk she saw the young family standing outside the door and knew instinctively that this was the family Vicente had been living with for the past months. As they neared she could see the young mother in the dim, yellow light reflected from the parking lot bulbs, concern showing on her pretty face.

Sylvia broke her grip on Pete's arm as they approached and stepped directly in front of Jessie. She wrapped her arms around the younger woman and hugged while patting her on the back.

The tears once again sprang freely from Jessie's eyes. "I'm so sorry."

The shorter woman, dark, slightly graying hair tied in a bun, released and stepped back just far enough to look up into Jessie's face. She lovingly patted her cheek. "It's okay, *Mi Hija*. It is in God's hands now."

Román introduced Ricky, Jessie and the kids and solemn handshakes were shared. He asked, "Can you tell us what happened?"

Jessie looked up at Ricky but it was obvious he was going to let her tell the story. She held her husband's hand and shuddered at the remembrance.

"I don't know the whole story. I just know he saved Jewell." She motioned toward the girl standing next to Jimmy Ray. "I had gone to get the mail then ran back when I saw the smoke. When I got to the clearing I saw him staggering from the house." She paused and chewed her lip. "He was on fire, really on fire. He brought Jewell away from the house in a rug that was also on fire. He unrolled her to safety then fell back. I got there as soon as I could but there was nothing... ." Her breath caught. "Nothing I could do."

Ricky reached to pull her close and Sylvia touched her lovingly on the shoulder.

Grim-faced the group entered as Ricky held the door and they walked directly to the Burn Center. A nurse called Dr. Ruiz who was working late that day. He shook the father's limp hand and allowed the mother to embrace him. All waited for the report though everyone could see that he was hesitant to give it.

"It's all right," volunteered Vicente's dad, pulling his wife close. "Tell us the truth."

Dr. Ruiz shook his head and looked at the hardwood floor shining in the glare of the overhead lighting. Finally, he reached to take Sylvia's hand and hold Pete's elbow. "He was burned very severely. It is surprising to all of us that he's alive but he's a fighter. Still, I have to tell you that his chances of survival are very slim."

The doctor and Pete steadied Sylvia. She bravely recovered some composure and asked, "May we see him?"

"Of course. Please come this way."

The doctor led the parents and Román down the hall and into the room. He remained with them only a short time before grimly nodding at the mother then leaving them alone. Sylvia tightly grasped the metal railing of the bed at her son's side. Leaning close but careful not to touch the bandages for fear of causing additional damage, she leaned forward to touch her forehead on the pillow next to Vicente's head. After resting there a moment while the men waited, she stood, crossed herself, then wrapped her arms around her husband's neck and buried her face into his chest. Román, with his hat in his hand, carefully backed out of the room to allow them to grieve together.

***

The little family was sitting in hard-backed chairs in the reception area when they were joined by Román who pulled a chair to sit directly in front. No one spoke, there was nothing to say.

After a long, silent and uncomfortable hour they were joined by the boy's parents. Ricky and Román stood as the couple approached.

Jessie looked up into Sylvia's eyes but quickly glanced away, unable to hold the gaze because of the guilt she felt. In an instant, the perceptive Hispanic woman leaned and held Jessie's face in both hands. They looked deep into each other's eyes, the sadness and remorse plain to see. Finally, Sylvia lightly patted Jessie's cheek. "Will you come to the chapel and pray with us?"

Tears once again rolled down the younger woman's cheek and she bravely nodded her reply. Arm in arm the two mothers strolled down the hall into the main lobby then on to the chapel located on the first floor. The two children and five adults were the only ones in the good sized room. They sat on benches and each in their own way, prayed for Vicente, and Jessie also prayed for his parents in this time of crisis in their lives.

No one spoke for quite some time. Finally, Pete cleared his throat then said, "Thank you for letting Vicente come and stay with you. We tried to do what we could but he was running with the wrong crowd."

Ricky and Jessie both watched the disheartened, worried man. They knew only that much of the story but nothing more. "We're glad he could come. He's a good boy and was a lot of help."

Jessie flinched again at her guilt of the way she had treated him. Ricky had tried to tell her that the boy was coming around but she had refused to listen. Then she was stung even more severely by the man's next words.

"It all started the day the Marines arrived in their dress blue uniforms." The man got a faraway look in his eye as he continued the story. "It was a Saturday afternoon. Sylvia, Vicente and I were home watching a game on TV. The house was open and through the screen door we heard their car come to a stop on the street in front of our house.

They were so dignified and solemn as they approached the door." He paused to glance at his wife. "Sylvia and I knew right away what it meant but Vicente had no clue. They said he had died as a hero and that his actions had saved many. I suppose we should have taken some comfort in that but it's hard when you learn your son was killed. Vicente took it really hard. He didn't say a word, he just walked to his room and didn't come out for two hours. From that time he never mentioned Antonio again."

***

Sylvia gazed lovingly at her husband then crossed herself before glancing toward the young mother in the next chair. She could see on her face an ever-deepening sadness. She reached for her hand and held it on her lap.

"*Mi Hija*, I have something to show you."

Reaching into her oversized purse that she had been carrying on her shoulder since getting off the plane less than two hours earlier, she extracted an envelope. "Do you know how much he loved it at the ranch?" she questioned.

Jessie looked down and rubbed the stiff denim of the new pants just for something to do with her free hand. She was thankful that Ricky reached for her then offered the answer.

"He wasn't very talkative but we knew he was beginning to feel at home there. He helped on the ranch welding and fixing vehicles. He even helped one of our neighbors with their truck."

Sylvia nodded while extracting pages from the envelope. She slowly unfolded them and pressed her fingers over the creases. "Here is his last letter to us. Would you read it please?" She pushed the papers toward Ricky though she was intent on watching Jessie the entire time.

Ricky solemnly took the papers and started reading.

"Out loud, please," Sylvia requested.

He cleared his throat and started from the top.

Mom and Dad,

I've been such a fool. I want you to know that I love you both and that I'm sorry for the pain I have caused you. I don't know what I was thinking but I want you to know that I've had a chance to learn things I never would have been willing to learn in LA. Not that you didn't try to teach me and I feel terrible that I treated you the way I did. I could have learned so much from you and now that I'm willing to admit it, I really did learn a lot. I learned how important it is to treat people right, to be honest and fair and to always stand up for what you believe in. I knew those things but was too stupid to remember them. I know you tried and it's all my fault for not listening to you. If it's okay with you I'd like to come home for a visit in a couple of weeks and when I do I'll be the kind of son you always wanted me to be.

I've come to love the ranch and the people here and quite honestly I could be happy here the rest of my life. In fact, before I come home for a visit I'll talk with *Patrón* Ricky to see if I could come back and keep working for him. I love the wide open spaces here and I love that I get to help people. I've been working on a family's old truck and their appreciation is my only reward but to tell the truth, it is better than money.

I got to see first-hand what it is like to care for your neighbor. The other night *Patrón* Ricky woke us up to go search for a little girl that was missing. It was a cold, dark night and almost everyone in the whole valley showed up to help. They didn't ask for pay and came even if it would have been easier to stay home.

I searched like the rest and I can't tell you how

good it felt to be accepted by the folks here. I was lucky enough to be the one that found her. That's how I met Gabriella. She is the sister to the lost girl and she is the sweetest, kindest and smartest girl I've ever met. She wants to go to college but can't go in Texas. Does Uncle Larry still work at the college in the foothills? Is there a way you could talk to him and see what it would take for her to go to school in California? Her problem is that she is illegal but that shouldn't be a problem there. At least it wasn't a problem for the Jimenez brothers that I went to school with. I'd love it if we could help Gabriella. It would mean a lot to me.

Patrón Ricky is a good boss and he trusts me which is a good feeling. I'm ashamed to admit that I wasn't very trustworthy when I first got here but somewhere along the line I decided that I wanted to be like you, Dad. Someone that could be trusted no matter what and I've tried to be that way. Thank you for being such a good example and I'm sorry again that I wasn't that way at home.

His wife's name is Jessie and she doesn't like me very much though I'll be the first to admit that I've given her every reason to feel that way. I'm hoping in time that she can forgive me for treating her badly.

They have two kids, Jimmy Ray and Jewell. They are good kids. Jimmy Ray wants someday to see an ocean. Maybe if he ever comes to LA I can take him.

I'm looking forward to seeing you in a couple of weeks. I'll call from the house sometime next week. It will be good to hear your voices. Being away was hard but I can finally see the

wisdom in your sending me to Román's. I miss you lots.
Love, Vicente

Chapter 25

The tears dripped silently from Jessie's cheeks to her new pants. She felt Sylvia reaching to her, touching her cheek and lifting her face to look into her eyes. The two women reached for each other and embraced.

"Ahem."

Everyone in the chapel turned to see Dr. Ruiz. "Excuse me," he said in a quiet, reserved voice. "I wanted to let you know that his lungs are filling with fluid. I'm afraid it won't be long now."

Sylvia stood and stepped to her husband's side holding tightly to his elbow. Resigned, they followed the doctor into the hall toward the burn center. Jessie stood also holding tightly to Ricky and together they, along with Román, Jimmy Ray and Jewell, watched the grieving couple walk away to be with their dying son.

***

Jewell tugged her mother's blouse. "Mom, I'm really tired."

Jessie quickly bent to hold her daughter, shuddering at the recurring thought that if not for Vicente she and Ricky would be the grieving parents.

Román, standing at the side, turned to the young couple. "I'll stay here. You guys go get some sleep. I'll take care of Sylvia and Pete." He reached to touch Jessie on the shoulder. "I'm sorry this happened but I'm happy that Jewell is all right."

She placed her hand on his as it rested on her shoulder and looked sadly into his eyes. "I was so mean to him," she whispered.

Román glanced at Ricky then focused on the young mother. "You have nothing to be ashamed of. You opened your home to him during a time in his life when he wasn't receptive. You allowed him to grow and learn at a great inconvenience to you. You and Ricky brought meaning to his life. He may die but remember this, the man he is today is not the boy that first came to live with you. You gave a great gift to his parents, the gift of remembering their son as a fine young man who was valued and loved."

The tears flowed freely down her cheeks as she reached to hug this wise man who had become such a friend.

"Thank you," she said as she stepped back and took Ricky's hand.

Román nodded then spoke to his young cowboy friend. "Sylvia and Pete have some decisions to make. I'll get them to a motel so they can rest too. Let's meet back here at 11:00 o'clock tomorrow morning then you can go back to the ranch. You've got some decisions to make also and some work to do with the insurance companies."

"We don't have to rush back. Scott is in the bunkhouse taking care of things."

Román noticed the children standing quietly at their parent's side. "But you'll need the bunkhouse to live in while your house is rebuilt. Scott can come back to Roswell to stay with me. Tomorrow's Sunday so let's think about it tonight and decide what to do tomorrow."

Ricky nodded silently then the little family, holding hands, walked down the halls to the front door and out of the hospital.

***

Román watched his cousin and her husband as they sat quietly on a plush leather couch in the burn center lounge waiting for Ricky and his family to arrive. He had arranged for a room at a nearby hotel but knew that neither had slept much the previous night. Their exhaustion mixed with grief was plain on their faces. He wondered how they could be so composed and then in an instant thought was thankful that his daughters were safe at home and he prayed that he would never have to endure an ordeal such as the one his relatives were facing.

He heard the footsteps on the hardwood floor before the young family turned the corner, then watched as Sylvia stood and immediately hugged Jessie. It seemed as though the older woman, the one that needed the consolation, was actually giving rather than receiving.

Román blinked at the sudden realization that both of these women needed consolation but it wasn't about giving and receiving, it was about sharing in the loss and sharing in the determination to move forward. He shook his head as he watched the two fathers shake hands and decided that to a lesser degree it was the same for them.

Sylvia stepped back to her husband's side then pulled the letter once again from her purse. She held it for all to see. The room was silent as all waited for her to speak. "We've been thinking about how much Vicente loved the ranch. Since he wanted to go back there we were wondering if it would be okay with you if he was buried in the little cemetery he told us about. He mentioned in one of our phone calls that he had painted the fence and it was such a quiet and beautiful place."

The young couple was stunned but quickly agreed. "We'd be proud to have him there," answered Ricky with a nod.

Román watched, surprised. That was the last thing he was expecting but at the thought decided that burying the boy on the ranch would be a fitting tribute. It was, after all, the place he had found himself, the place he had done a lot of growing up.

***

The days leading up to the funeral had been hectic for

Ricky and Jessie. There were calls to their workman's comp insurance carrier to pay for the air ambulance ride and the hospital stay in Lubbock as well as their home insurance about rebuilding the house. An unexpected outcome was that the home insurance sent a check for $10,000 for Vicente's parents to help with funeral and other expenses.

There were calls to the government offices for permission to bury the boy in the ranch cemetery and calls to local contractors to get started on a new house.

Since the closest motel was an hour away they and the kids had been invited to stay with their good friend and neighbor, Bob, for a few days until things settled at the ranch. When the former state senator learned that Pete and Sylvia also needed a place to stay for a few days he graciously volunteered.

On the afternoon before the graveside service, Pete and Sylvia were sitting on a balcony which jutted from the second story of the house overlooking acres and acres of west Texas grassland turning green in the springtime warmness. They sat side-by-side in white-painted metal chairs, holding hands. Neither spoke, they simply sat staring off into the distance.

Sylvia rubbed her husband's hand. When he glanced at her she said, "It will be hard to go back to our house. It will seem so empty and cold."

He nodded then returned his gaze to the faraway hills, slowly rocking back and forth in the chair.

Another long moment passed before she spoke again. "He wanted us to help the girl. What if she came to live with us?"

He offered no answer but stood to lean on the railing for a full minute while she waited patiently. Finally, he turned. "We don't even know them. We don't know anything about them."

She was quiet then joined him at the railing. "Then let's get to know them. He wanted us to help. Let's do it for him."

He reached for her hand again then pulled her close for an embrace. At length, she pushed away and gazed up into his face. He touched her cheek then nodded sadly.

Below them they heard a sound. They watched with interest as Bob walked through the lawn at the front of the house. Pete leaned both hands on the railing. "Excuse me."

Bob looked up, holding his hand to shade his eyes from the overhead sun. "Hi, Pete. What can I do for you?"

Pete lifted his palms and shrugged. "You've already done so much. We just wanted to express our appreciation. But, if it wouldn't be too much trouble, we'd like to ask you a question." He waved, inviting their newfound friend to join them.

Bob nodded then stepped directly to the stairs at the side of the house that led to the balcony. Once at the top he pulled a matching chair to their side and sat. "Ask away."

Pete held Sylvia's hand while they sat in the chairs. The couple focused on each other for the briefest moment then both turned to Bob. Pete asked, "Can you tell us something about the Reyes family?"

A big grin formed on Bob's face. He leaned back, got comfortable and said, "What can I tell you about them? Well, I can tell you that they are a fine family, honest as the day is long and always the first to volunteer when help is needed. Rosalinda and the girls come every other week to help my wife with house chores and Juan and the boys have been here many times to help me with various projects. I'm proud to call them my friends."

The couple smiled at the answer then exchanged glances before Sylvia spoke. "Vicente said that Gabriella wants to go to college?"

"I wouldn't know about that but if she does she'll do well I'm sure."

"There was some problem. Some reason she couldn't go to school in Texas. Something about having to pay out-of-state tuition because she's not legal."

Bob suddenly frowned at the recollection of the years

of heated debates at the legislature about that very topic. It was a very sensitive issue and he could see the merits of the arguments from both sides. "Yes," he agreed, understanding the current law. "Unless she can prove legal status she'll have to pay out-of-state tuition if she attends a Texas college or university."

"So her chances of attending college here are pretty much zero?"

The frown continued as he nodded his agreement to the statement.

All three stared out into the distance. Finally, Pete turned to Sylvia and noticing her nod of encouragement, continued, "Vicente wanted us to see if there was a chance she could go to college in California since the tuition at community colleges there is inexpensive. What do you think?"

Bob scratched a small nick in the paint on the arm of his chair while he was thinking. At length, he looked up. "California is a long ways away for a girl that has lived in this little valley her whole life. She's a good girl and I hear she's really smart but that's an awfully big step to expect her to go out there on her own. Shucks, she's probably never even been to a city bigger than San Angelo, and I'm not so sure she's ever been there." He looked into their faces and could see compassion and he hated to put a damper on their enthusiasm. "I can't help but think she would panic out there on her own."

The couple both studied their shoes for a long while. Finally, Sylvia concentrated on Bob. "We were thinking of inviting her to live with us. Our home is small but we have an extra bedroom now." Tears showed in her eyes. "Vicente really liked her and we'd like to do something. You said the family is a good family and she's a good girl. We'd love to be able to help."

***

The bright and clear spring day of the graveside service arrived. Many of the people from the valley attended even though they hardly knew Vicente, but they knew the Richardson family and attended out of respect for them and out of gratitude that the boy had given his life to save Jewell.

The parents solemnly shook hands as the crowd passed by. Sylvia noticed out of the corner of her eye a thin girl with long, black hair and knew immediately that it was the girl Vicente had written about. As she approached in the line they shook hands but Gabriella was pulled close for an unexpected hug.

"*Su estoy* Gabriella?" Sylvia whispered into her ear.

The surprised girl answered, also in Spanish. "Yes, I am Gabriella."

"When the service is over we must talk. Will you please stay and bring your parents?"

"Of course." She walked away while looking over her shoulder with a bewildered expression.

Sylvia surveyed the small crowd gathered around the casket, most uncomfortably studying their boots or shoes, men with hats in hands and women standing stoically alongside. She then scanned the horizon and felt an inexplicable calmness come over her along with a feeling of oneness with this valley and the people that lived here. She could see how her son could come to love this place in such a short time.

The service was short. As the crowd slowly drifted away she was happy to see that Ricky and Jessie shook hands with each attendee, expressing appreciation that they had come. She looked around, wondering where the girl had gone but was relieved when she noticed her, her parents and possibly a little sister standing at the side with obvious respect. Sylvia took her husband's arm. Together they moved away from the grave toward the family.

The men shook hands and the women, though strangers until that moment, hugged like long-lost friends. Introductions were exchanged in Spanish then Sylvia explained the reason they had chosen to have Vicente buried at the ranch. "He told us he loved this place and the people here and he mentioned you, Gabriella, several times."

The young girl, embarrassed at the conversation, looked down and away.

Sylvia continued, "We understand you would like to go to college. Is that right?"

Gabriella quickly searched the woman's face with instant curiosity, then at once retreated into reticent stoicism. "Yes but I probably won't," she admitted with a frown.

Sylvia reached to take her hand and held it even though it seemed to make the girl uncomfortable. "There is a way if you're interested. It was Vicente's wish that we help you go to college. Are you interested in hearing how it could happen?"

Gabriella glanced at her parents. It was obvious she was interested. At a nod from her mother, she turned back to Sylvia in reserved anticipation. "How much did he tell you about my situation?" she asked.

"We know that your finances will not allow you to attend college in Texas," volunteered the California woman hoping that the girl would understand that they knew she was illegal without having to say it out loud.

Gabriella nodded grimly, plainly discerning the meaning. "Yes, that is true."

"California is not as afraid of immigrants as Texas seems to be. I have a brother who works for a college in the foothills. He said if you lived with us you could go there for in-state tuition and he thinks he can find a scholarship for you. Our house is empty now and we would love for you to come to LA when you graduate in May."

Gabriella's cheeks flushed at the thought, and though all could see she was plainly interested she politely answered, "I could never accept. I would be too much of a burden."

"Nonsense. Our house is empty and we'd love to have

you come. You don't have to make up your mind right away but you let us know so we can put you in contact with my brother." Sylvia released the girl's hand then turned to her parents. "You don't know us yet but she is welcome and we'll treat her as our own daughter. Please let her come."

Rosalinda leaned forward, grinning. "Come to our house for lunch and stay the afternoon. We can become acquainted. I'll think we'll be good friends."

Sylvia returned the grin then after a nod from her husband, said, "We'll be happy to. I've already had too much restaurant food, we need a good meal."

Rosalinda laughed loudly, held her long skirt out of the grass with one hand and Sylvia's arm with the other. "Then let's go. You can help me with the tortillas while the men brag to each other about meaningless trivialities."

***

The July sun shone brightly on a Saturday morning in the little valley between San Angelo and Abilene. Ricky rode the buckskin colt that was doing so well he could hardly be considered a colt any longer while Jimmy Ray rode Pardner through the green and growing grass in the pastures. They had been checking on the cows to make sure all was good and both were enjoying their time together.

At a hilltop, the pair stopped and gazed down on the new fence that had been completed only a few months earlier. It was straight, tight and true, a fence to be proud of. At the sight, they both thought of Vicente. Ricky smiled sadly at the recollection of the change that had come about in the youngster's life.

They sat silently for a long moment before Ricky commented wistfully to his son. "He was a good boy."

Jimmy Ray leaned back and patted the big black horse on the hip while watching his dad chew the inside of his cheek. Finally, with wisdom beyond his 12 years, said, "I think we all learned something from him."

Ricky turned to his son, the saddle creaking from the movement. Reaching out he squeezed the boy's shoulder.

"Yes," he said. "We all learned something from him." Turning the colt he pointed forward with his nose, toward a huge oak tree on a distant hill. "Let's ride back past the cemetery."

At a comfortable half-trot the two horses covered the country. As they approached they noticed someone else there. When they got close enough they realized it was Gabriella. She was leaning on the fence staring in at the grave now covered with native grass. The man and boy joined her, leaning on their saddle horns just outside the white picket fence.

"Hi, Gabriella," they both said in unison.

"Hi," she replied looking up at them with a reserved smile. "I wanted to stop and visit one last time before I leave to California. I hope you don't mind?"

"Happy to have you here," said Ricky without hesitation. "When do you leave?"

"Tomorrow morning. My brother Alfonso will drive me to San Angelo where I'll get on a bus. I'm scared and excited at the same time."

"I can understand that. Good luck to you."

"Thanks. I'm so glad his parents invited me to live with them. My folks fell in love with them right away and they stayed in contact over the last months. I can't believe it but I'm going to college!" She shook her head and the smile expanded.

Ricky glanced at his son and enjoyed the smile he saw returned from the young face. He turned to the girl. "Yes, you are and good for you. You be careful out there."

"Oh, I will." She leaned back and shook her head causing her hair to fall behind her shoulders before turning back to look over the white picket fence. "When did the headstone get here?" she asked while pointing to the inscribed, gray marble slab.

"The company just set it a few weeks ago. What do you think?"

"I like it," she answered. "It speaks the truth."

"Yes, it does," agreed the ranchman as he reread the inscription, dark and deep in the stone.

VICENTE ZERMENO
1987 – 2016
A GOOD MAN GONE

The End

Author's note: In my little Southeastern Arizona town we have more than a few kids sent from LA to live with their grandparents or uncles and aunts to give them a chance away from bad influences. Some take advantage of the situation while sadly, others don't. Here's to those that learn, grow and develop as productive young people.

About the Author

Randall Dale grew up in a ranching family. No stranger to long days in the saddle, Randall draws heavily on his experiences to bring a new breed of western novels. He is a graduate of The University of Arizona and while there was a member of the rodeo and livestock judging teams. He is a past champion of the United States Team Roping Championships and continues to compete when time permits.

Randall is a devoted family man and successful businessman with a flair for writing, and an interest in all things western. He currently lives in rural Southeastern Arizona with his wife. They enjoy spending time with their children and grandchildren.

Please feel free to email with any thoughts, comments or even suggested story lines for future books. I'd love to hear from you.
randall@randalldale.com

Made in the USA
San Bernardino, CA
13 December 2016